THE JUMBO BOOK OF

SCIENCE

136 of the Best Experiments from the Ontario Science Centre

KIDS CAN PRESS LTD.

Toronto

The Ontario Science Centre is an agency of the Government of Ontario.

Kids Can Press Ltd. acknowledges with appreciation the assistance of the Canada Council and the Ontario Arts Council in the production of this book.

Canadian Cataloguing in Publication Data

Main entry under title:

The Jumbo book of science : 136 of the best experiments from the Ontario Science Centre

Includes index.
ISBN 1–55074–197–7
1. Science – Experiments – Juvenile literature.
I. Hendry, Linda.   II. Cupples, Patricia.
III. Holdcroft, Tina.   IV. Ontario Science Centre.

Q164.J85 1994   j500   C93–095513–7

Kids Can Press Ltd.
29 Birch Avenue
Toronto, Ontario, Canada
M4V 1E2

Text stock contains
over 50% recycled paper

94 0 9 8 7 6 5 4 3 2 1

Written by Carol Gold, with
   Mary Donev, Stef Donev and
   Hugh Westrup
Edited by Valerie Wyatt
Designed by N.R. Jackson and
   Michael Solomon
Cover designed by N.R. Jackson
Printed and bound in Canada

The material in this book originally appeared in *Scienceworks, Foodworks* and *How Sport Works.*

ILLUSTRATION CREDITS

Pat Cupples:
cover, 6–7, 10–13, 17–35, 50–51, 62–63, 80–81, 96–97, 106–11, 114–17, 120–29, 136–41, 166–87

Linda Hendry:
36–49, 76–77, 82–83, 86–89, 91–95, 130–31, 148–53, 155

Tina Holdcroft:
8–9, 14–16, 52–61, 64–75, 78–79, 84–85, 90, 98–99, 101–5, 112–13, 118–19, 132–35, 142–47, 154, 156–65, 188

TABLE OF CONTENTS

THE GREAT OUTDOORS 96

SCIENCE WHATS, HOWS AND WHYS 114

THINGS TO MAKE 140

THE SCIENCE OF FUN 166

ACKNOWLEDGEMENTS

The Ontario Science Centre books couldn't happen without the knowledge, ideas, patience and commitment of many people. Among them are the following: Judy Arrowood, Jamie Bell, Randy Betts, Peter Birnbaum, Julie Bowen, Lorraine Brown, Allan Busch, Bruce Crabe, Luigia Dedivitiis, Marici Dillon, Debra Feldman, Elisabeth Frecaut, Jeffrey Golde, Eric Grace, Daryl Gray, Becky Hall, Valerie Hatten, Kim Humphreys, Judy Janzen, Thom Jenkins, Jerry Krause, Martin Leek, Jennifer Martin, Hooley McLaughlin, Ron Miller, Jennifer Murray, OSC Host Group, Linda Pacheco, Gary Pattenden, Gary Renaud, Bill Robinson, Ivan Semeniuk, Grant Slinn, David Spence, Cathie Spencer, David Steeper, David Sugarman, Earl Sweeney, Chris Szweda, Paul Terry, Patrick Tevlin, Roberta Tevlin, Vic Tyrer, Tony Vander Voet, George Vanderkuur, Kevin Von Appen, Carol White and the entire staff of the Ontario Science Centre, each of whom, in his or her own way, has made these books possible.

BODY SCIENCE

A MYSTERY AT YOUR FINGERTIPS

Do you ever suspect that someone's been in your room without asking permission? Here's a simple fingerprinting experiment to help you finger the culprit.

You'll need:
a stamp pad
a piece of white paper
talcum powder
a fine paintbrush
clear cellophane tape
shiny black paper (dark blue will work too, but not as well)

1. Before anyone becomes suspicious, get a record of all possible suspects' fingerprints. Have each person press the pads of his or her fingers, one at a time, onto an ink pad, then roll the inky fingers on a piece of paper laid flat on a hard surface. In order to get the entire pattern, you have to roll the finger instead of just pressing it down flat.
2. Examine the prints. You may already know that each person's fingerprints are different from everyone else's, but does each person have the same print on all their fingers?
3. Now it's time to see if you can match a suspect's fingerprints with fingerprints in your room. Dust the talcum powder lightly on several hard surfaces in your room such as a desk, a light switch, and the doorknob.
4. Blow on the talcum powder gently so that most of the powder blows away, except for spots where the powder sticks to fingerprints and other greasy marks.

5. To reveal the prints, brush the powdered spots very lightly with your fine paintbrush until the pattern shows. It may take some practice until you learn to brush enough to reveal the pattern without damaging the print.

6. If you want to examine the fingerprint or keep it, you can lift it by pressing a piece of sticky tape over it, then peeling the tape away with the powder pattern on it. Stick the tape on the shiny black paper and the print will show up very clearly.

7. Now compare the fingerprints you collected from your suspects with the ones you found in your room. If any of them match, you've probably found the culprit.

What are fingerprints?

If you look at your skin under a microscope, you'll see that it has many tiny holes, called pores, through which oil and perspiration reach the surface and evaporate. When you touch anything, the oil and perspiration on the ridges of your fingers leave an invisible print. Fine powder sticks to the faint, oily finger deposits and reveals the prints of the people who left them.

This method of finding and lifting fingerprints is the one that's been used since Sir Francis Galton founded it in the mid-1800s.

HAVE you ever been walking along the street and suddenly tripped over nothing? Your friends look at you and sneer, "Walk much?"

What happened?

To find out, find an out-of-the way spot (preferably grass, because it's softer) where you can lie on your stomach and watch people walk by.

How high do they lift their feet off the ground?

Are you a daisy clipper?

When you walk through a field of daisies, do your feet clip the tops off the flowers?

That's what people used to look for when buying horses or dogs if they needed speed or endurance over long distances. An animal that barely lifts its feet off the ground (a daisy clipper) doesn't waste energy that instead can be used for doing the chores (hunting, racing, sheep herding, pulling a wagon). Today, there are more sophisticated ways of measuring how high an animal lifts its feet, but the best animals are still those who'd clip the heads off daisies.

The opposite of a daisy clip is a hackney stride. Perhaps you've seen horses that pick up their feet in a dainty, prancing gait. That's a hackney stride. It may look pretty but it's definitely not energy efficient.

Now, from your observations, do people make good daisy clippers? They should. Most pedestrians clear the ground by only about 1 cm (⅓ inch). Walking in this way is energy efficient—you don't do any more work than is necessary.

Unfortunately it doesn't take more than a little rise in the concrete for a daisy clipper to stub a toe. And then it's, "Walk much?"

Are you a floater?

Go back to your foot observation post and focus your attention on any joggers passing by. Can you tell the difference between the gait of a runner and a walker?

Runners "float." They spend part of the time with both feet off the ground. And the faster they run, the more time both feet are airborne. Walkers, on the other hand—er, foot—always have at least one foot on the ground. See if you can sense this difference as you compare yourself running and walking. Do you feel yourself "float"?

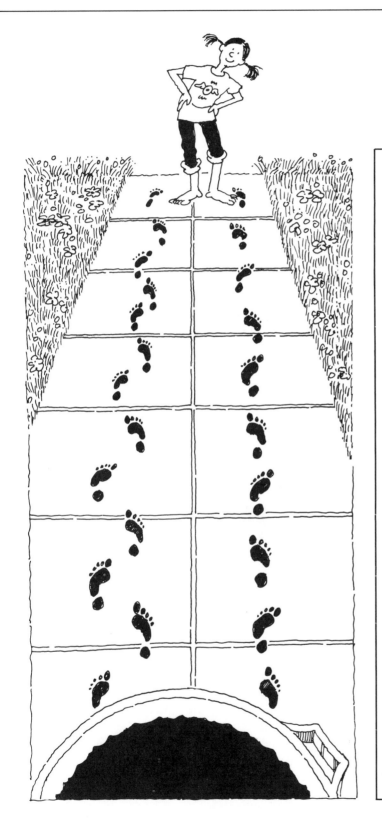

Footprint detective

Can you tell the difference between the tracks of someone running or walking?

You'll need:
two bare feet
a sidewalk
a tub of water

1. Get your feet good and soaking wet.
2. Walk down the sidewalk. Look back at your tracks on the concrete.
3. Soak your feet again and run down the walk. Notice any difference between your walking and running footprints?

When you walk, your feet move parallel to each other, as if moving on two side-by-side tracks. When running, they follow one another, as if on a tightrope, making a single track.

Like daisy clipping, "single tracking" is an energy-saver. When your legs move on parallel tracks, you sway from side to side as you switch legs, which wastes energy. You have to use the parallel-track system when you walk in order to keep your balance. (Think how difficult it is to walk putting one foot directly in front of the other.) But it's easier to maintain your balance when you move faster, so you can manage with just one leg at a time right underneath the centre of your body. The energy you save by not swaying can be used to move your legs forward faster. To see how well it works, try running with your legs making parallel tracks.

OU'LL need:
a friend whose feet are the same size as yours
her well-used shoes

1. Put on your friend's shoes and have her put on yours.
2. Go for a walk.

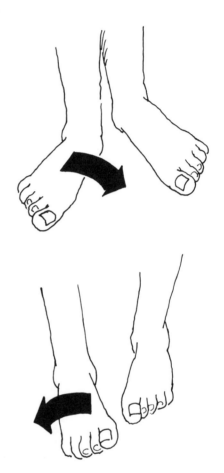

Feel awkward? Find your feet moving a little differently than usual? That's because well-worn shoes are the leather memory of their owner's gait. Put them on and they force you to walk the way she does. And everyone has a slightly different gait.

A normal footstep advances smoothly, beginning at the heel and rolling forward to a firm lift-off at the toes. Your foot comes down on the outer edge of your heel, then rolls forward on what would be the skinny part of your footprint, then inward to the ball of your foot.

If your foot has a tendency to roll farther inward toward your big toe as it moves to push off, this is called pronation. If your foot rolls outward as it pushes off, you supinate. Most people pronate slightly and this is why the average person walks with slightly turned-out feet.

But some people have really exaggerated rolls—they **overpronate** or **oversupinate**. Both types of people look a little like birds: overpronators walk in a duck gait; oversupinators are pigeon-toed.

Play Sherlock Holmes with Your Shoes

How do you walk?

Turn your shoes over and examine the wear and tear on your soles. If you've worn down the outside rim of your soles, you're a supinator. If you've worn down the inside of your soles you're a pronator. Or maybe you fall (or should we say walk?) somewhere in between.

TWO EYES ARE BETTER THAN ONE

DID you ever wonder why you need two eyes? One reason is that they help you see depth. To find out how different your depth perception would be with only one eye, try this experiment with a friend.

You'll need:
a cup
a penny

1. Put the cup on the table and stand about 3 m (9 feet) away.
2. Cover one eye. Have your friend hold the penny at arm's length above the cup, but slightly in front of it.
3. Watching only the cup and the penny, tell your friend where to move his arm so that the penny will fall into the cup when he drops it.
4. Tell him to drop the penny and see how close you came. Why are you such a bad shot?

How does it work?
Because our eyes are set apart from each other, they see everything from slightly different angles. So the images your brain gets from each eye are a little different from one another. By comparing the images, your brain can give you a three-dimensional picture which helps you judge distances. This is called stereoscopic vision. When you cover one eye, you no longer have stereoscopic vision and you see things in two dimensions, like a photograph. This makes judging distances much more difficult.

Fortunately, there are other clues to help you judge depth in real life, such as size, brightness, and position compared to other familiar objects. These are the clues that people use if they lose the sight in one eye. You can improve your one-eyed depth perception too. Try the penny drop test several times. You'll soon be hitting the cup quite easily.

FOOL YOUR SENSES

AN a bowl of water be hot and cold at the same time? Try this easy experiment and find out.

You'll need:
3 bowls

1. Pour cold water into one bowl, hot water into another, and lukewarm water into the third.
2. Dunk one hand into the cold water and the other into the hot water and leave them there for a minute or two.
3. Put both hands together into the lukewarm bowl. The lukewarm water will feel hot to one hand and cold to the other at the same time!

How does it work?
The hand that was in the cold water feels the medium temperature as hot; the hand that was in the hot water feels it as cold. You're experiencing sensory adaptation. That's what happens when any of your senses is exposed to the same strong sensation for a while. Your sense receptors get used to it and stop sending reports to your brain. That's why the good smell of dinner cooking is so powerful when you walk into the house, but fades away after you've been inside a few minutes. It's only when the sensation changes that you notice it again.

Sometimes your sense receptors can be fooled by dramatic changes and give you a false report, as in this experiment, where each hand feels the water as being the opposite to the temperature the hand was used to.

DID you know that you can make a hot and cold map on your body?

You'll need:
2 fine-tipped felt pens of different colours
a bowl
a nail

1. Draw a box about 2 cm square (1 inch square) on the back of your hand with one of the felt pens.
2. Fill the bowl with cold water and set the nail in it until it's cold to the touch.
3. Touch the tip of the cold nail to any spot inside the square. If it feels cold, mark the spot with one of the pens. Try other places inside the square, marking the ones that feel cold with the same colour. You'll probably have to keep putting the nail back into the water to keep it cold.
4. When you've tested the entire square for cold, heat the nail in hot water and, with the other colour,

mark where you feel heat. If you touch a marked cold spot with the hot nail, can you feel it? When you've finished marking off all the heat and cold receptors in that square, examine the map you've made. Were there more hot spots or cold spots?

How does it work?
Scientists have found that our bodies have separate spots, called receptors, for feeling temperatures that are hotter or colder than body temperature. The two different colours of dots on your hand give a map of your own hot and cold receptors. Other areas of your body may produce different maps. Try mapping small squares on your forehead, fingers, chin, palm, forearm, and the sole of your foot. You might find out the best way to pick up a snowball without feeling the cold!

NO SWEAT

EY, you! You're just sitting there reading this book, taking it easy. No sweat, huh? Wrong, damp one. Take a close look.

You'll need:
a strong magnifying glass
a desk lamp

1. Make a fist with one of your hands for 10-15 seconds.
2. Open your hand and hold it, palm side up, under the light. Look carefully at the tips of your fingers through the magnifying glass.

Those tiny pieces of glitter on your fingertips are actually droplets of sweat catching the light.

Now that you've seen that even sitting and reading can make you sweat, how much sweat do you think you produce in a day? Well, if you relaxed in an air-conditioned movie theatre all day, you'd lose about a cup of sweat. Spend a hot day playing sports or just running around and you could produce almost a bucketful. Adult marathon runners can produce nearly three times that much in a single race. If they don't replace all that lost water throughout the competition, the results can be serious, especially if it's a hot day. You can actually lose so much water that your body stops perspiring, which can lead to heat exhaustion or deadly heatstroke.

If you just have to put all this water back, why get rid of it in the first place? Sweating is a water-cooling system. The engines of the human body, the muscles, produce a great deal of heat, which the body must eliminate to keep its temperature from rising to dangerous levels. During heavy exercise, muscles transfer their excess heat to the blood, which then rushes to the surface of the body. That's why some people get so red-looking when they exercise.

Meanwhile, the brain has instructed the pores of the skin to squeeze out droplets of water, which form the layer of sweat on the skin. When the hot blood reaches the surface of the body, its heat is immediately transferred to this sweaty layer. The heat is used up by evaporating the sweat. The more heat your body produces, the more sweat it needs to carry the heat away.

YOU'VE probably seen an aerobic workout. You know. . .designer gym togs, sweat bands and non-stop jumping jacks, bun lifts, froggy-ups and ham sandwiches. But have you ever seen an *anaerobic* workout? What's the difference? Try this test to find out.

You'll need:
a flight of stairs
a stopwatch or a watch with a second hand

1. Run up and down the stairs for 20 seconds. While you're running, notice how you're breathing.
2. After a short rest, run around the block at a steady pace. Notice how you're breathing this time. Was there any difference between the way you breathed in the two exercises?

"Aerobics" is a Greek word that roughly means "with air." Aerobic exercises are so-called because they require oxygen to produce the energy for rapid movement of the muscles. When you ran around the block, did you notice how heavily you were breathing? That's because your body required big gulps of oxygen. You were doing an aerobic exercise.

If aerobics means "with air," then "anaerobics" must mean—you guessed it—"without air." An anaerobic exercise is one that doesn't require oxygen for the production of energy. When you ran up and down the stairs, you didn't breathe as deeply as you did while circling the block. You were doing an anaerobic exercise.

Your body is able to produce energy without oxygen only during brief periods of intense activity. Anaerobic exercises never last for more than about two minutes. Once you pass the two-minute mark, your aerobic system starts to take over.

If you think about it, the anaerobic-to-aerobic system is a very clever mechanism. When the starting pistol fires and you bolt from the starting blocks, or when you meet a big grizzly bear in the bush and must run for your life, your lungs just can't breathe fast enough to meet your muscles' sudden high demand for oxygen. So you rely on a source of energy—anaerobic energy—that doesn't require oxygen, until your breathing catches up to the movement of your limbs.

Taking out stitches

Have you ever laughed so hard your sides ached? The pain you felt was the same as the kind of pain that you sometimes get in your side when you exercise too hard. Both pains are called stitches.

A stitch is a cramp in your diaphragm, the muscle that controls your breathing. During exercise (or laughter), the human diaphragm functions like any other hard-working muscle; sometimes it can tighten up and fail to relax, like an overworked leg with a charley horse.

The best treatment for a cramp is to stretch the muscle to its normal relaxed position and then massage it. Once the cramp is gone, you can go back to exercising—or laughing—though if the pain returns, it's probably best to stop for the day.

THIS SIDE UP

You probably don't think much about your sense of balance from day to day, though life is really one long balancing act. Every movement throws you at least a little off centre, putting you in danger of toppling over.

You'll need:
a full-length mirror
a ball of string
tape

1. Cut a piece of string the length of the mirror.
2. Tape one end to the centre of the mirror at the top and let it hang straight down. Tape the lower end of the string in place at the bottom of the mirror.

3. Stand in front of the mirror with your feet together and one eye closed and line up your nose with the string.
4. Lift your right leg just a little. Where does your nose go?
5. With your leg still hanging in the air, lift your left arm until it sticks straight out beside you. Where does your nose go now?

When you lifted your leg, your body was thrown off balance. That's why your nose (and the rest of you) shifted to the left — to keep you from falling over. Raising your left arm provided a counter-balance for your raised leg, and so your body moved back toward the centre.

Your arms and legs work to counterbalance each other just like two people on a teeter-totter. But because your legs are much heavier than your arms, it's like a fat kid and skinny kid sitting on the teeter-totter. Just as the skinny kid must sit farther out than the fat kid to keep the teeter-totter in balance, your arms must stick out farther than your legs to keep your body from tipping too far to one side.

How does your body keep adjusting its balance when you're always moving your legs and arms or shifting positions? By paying attention to a constant flood of messages from your eyes, joints and muscles. Like planes around a control tower, the eyes, joints and muscles are constantly letting your brain know where your limbs are located in relation to each other, and where you stand with respect to the ground.

But to make it all work, you need rocks in your head. And lucky for you, you have 'em. The rocks are actually tiny crystals and they're in two little hollow sacks, one near each eardrum. The sacks are lined with microscopic hairs. Whenever your body accelerates forward, or your head tilts to one

side, gravity causes the rocks to move, pressing against different hairs in the lining. Fast as lightning, the hairs relay a message to your brain, telling it about your change in position.

Are you well-balanced?
You'll need:
a watch with a second hand or a stopwatch
a friend

The Blind Stork Test
1. Put on running shoes and stand on a hard surface (not a rug). Get your friend ready with the watch.
2. Stand on your dominant leg (the one you kick with) and press your other foot against the knee of the leg you're standing on. Put your hands on your hips. Close your eyes.
3. As soon as your eyes are closed, your friend should start timing you with the watch. How long can you stand without shifting your foot or taking your hands off your hips or your foot off your knee?

This is a test of "static" balance. If you did well, you might make a good high diver or gymnast.

Hop till you Drop
1. Stand in stocking feet on a slick floor (e.g., tile or linoleum). Take the same position as for the first test but keep your eyes open this time.
2. Have your friend start the watch and tell you when five seconds has gone by. Then make a half turn by swivelling on the ball of your foot.
3. Keep turning every five seconds until you take your hands off your hips or your foot off your knee.

This is a test of "dynamic" balance. It shows how fine-tuned the muscle receptors in your legs are. If you did well, you might make a good surfer or downhill skier.

ELTOIDS, pectorals, trapezius and brachialis . . .

Is all of this Greek to you? Well, you're partly right. Most of the muscles in the human body have Greek or Latin names.

Athletes usually get so friendly with their muscles that they refer to them by their abbreviations: delts for deltoids, pecs for pectorals, and so on.

There are more than 600 skeletal muscles in the human body. The major ones are shown here. See if you can find them in your own body.

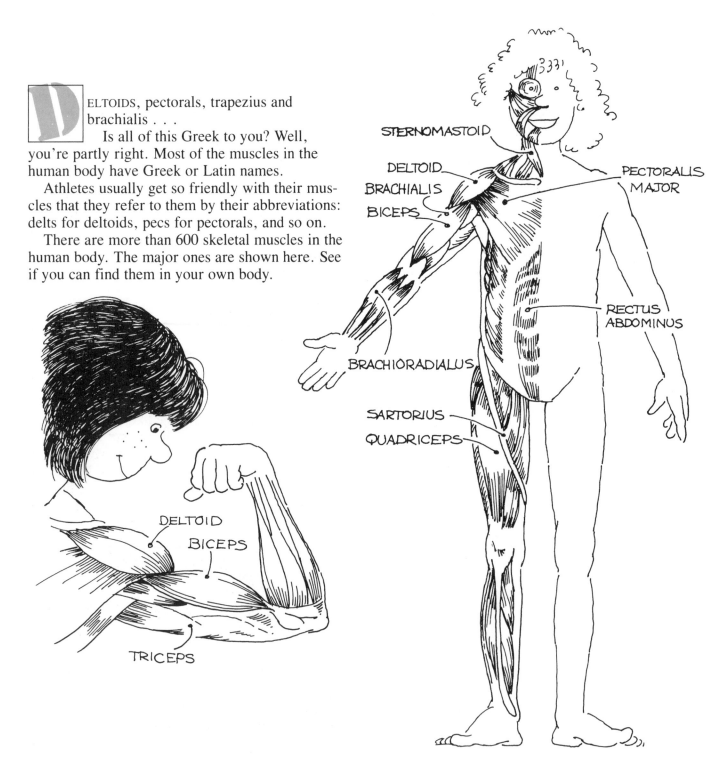

STERNOMASTOID

DELTOID

BRACHIALIS

BICEPS

PECTORALIS MAJOR

RECTUS ABDOMINUS

BRACHIORADIALUS

SARTORIUS

QUADRICEPS

DELTOID

BICEPS

TRICEPS

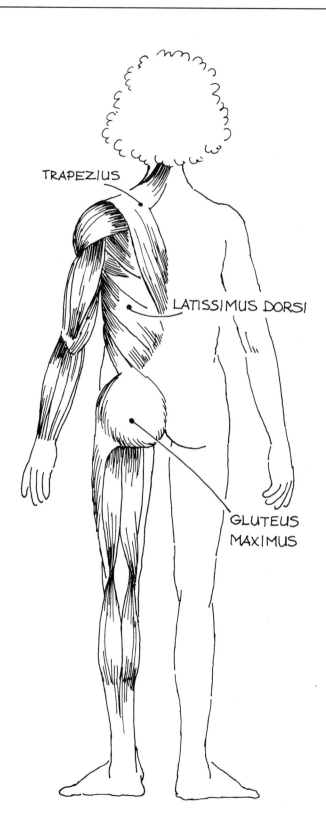

TRAPEZIUS

LATISSIMUS DORSI

GLUTEUS
MAXIMUS

Five fascinating facts about muscles

1. About 40 per cent of your body weight is muscle.
2. Your muscles are 75 per cent water! What's the rest? Twenty per cent is protein and the rest is assorted stuff such as salts, minerals and carbohydrates.

LEVATOR LABII SUPERIORIS
ALAEQUE NASI

3. One of the smallest muscles has one of the longest names. It's Levator labii superioris alaeque nasi. With a name like that, it should lift mountains, but it doesn't. It's the tiny muscle beside your nose that helps raise your lip into a sneer.
4. For their size, the muscles that operate the wings of bees, flies and mosquitoes are stronger than any human muscles.

5. Ever feel the hair standing up on your arms or neck? It's raised by tiny muscles pulling on each hair follicle.

Has anyone ever called you a turkey? Well, in one respect, they were right! Just like a turkey, you have white meat and dark meat.

If you were to extract some muscle tissue from your body and look at it under a microscope, you'd see a bunch of long, stringy fibres running side by side, like wires in a telephone cable. Some of the fibres would be richly supplied with blood; these make up the dark meat. The other fibres, which don't receive as much blood, would be the white meat.

Since you're not eating your muscles, but using them, you might not want to call them dark or white meat. Instead, you could use the names given them by scientists who study bodily changes during exercise. They call the white meat *fast-twitch fibres* and the dark meat *slow-twitch fibres*.

Fast-twitch fibres contract very quickly and yield a short burst of energy. You use your fast-twitch fibres whenever you make a sudden show of speed or strength.

Slow-twitch fibres, on the other hand, are used in sustained activities that don't require a flat-out display of effort, ones that last for more than about two minutes. Endurance sports, such as the marathon or cross-country skiing, are slow-twitch events. Most sports use a combination of these muscle fibres.

Everyone has the same overall number of fibres in each muscle, though the proportion of slow-twitch to fast-twitch fibres varies from person to person. You may have 80 per cent slow-twitch fibres and 20 per cent fast-twitch fibres, while your best friend has a 40-60 ratio. It's something you're born with and there's little you can do to change it.

Being born with more fast-twitch fibres endows you with a natural advantage in sprinting, while having more slow-twitch fibres gives you a head start in marathon racing. Alas, there's no way to count your fibres without surgically removing some of your muscle tissue.

Which Twitch Is Which?

You can't see your fast-twitch muscle fibres but here's how to feel their presence.

1. Stand with your back pressing against a wall and your feet planted about a step away from the wall.
2. Slide down the wall until you're almost in a sitting position. Hold yourself there for as long as you can. How do your legs feel?

That soreness in your thighs as you hold your position against the wall comes from a buildup of lactic acid, which is produced by fast-twitch muscle fibres when they're working. Lactic acid "gums up" the muscles, and must be constantly flushed out of your system. Sitting against the wall makes your thigh muscles so tense that the lactic acid cannot easily be removed and you feel pain. During heavy exercise, lactic acid can build up in your muscles in large quantities, which explains why you sometimes feel achy immediately after exercise. (The immediate achiness caused by lactic acid is different from the soreness that comes the day after exercise. The "next day" pain comes from microscopic tears in the muscle tissue caused by exercise.)

Warm Down

You've just finished three sets of tennis or several laps around the track and your immediate inclination is to sit down and rest.

Don't.

Follow exercise with a "warm down" period. Go for a five-minute walk, or do some stretching. Winding down gradually after exercise helps your circulation flush the excess lactic acid out of your muscles and reduces post-exercise soreness.

Fast-Twitch Food

It's a pain when lactic acid accumulates in your muscles, but you can eat it without any ill effects. The sour taste in plain yoghurt—that's lactic acid.

IF you've ever been to a circus or a carnival, you've no doubt gasped at the The Human Pretzel or The Snake Woman. These human wonders are so supple they can tie themselves in knots, or sit on their own head, or rotate their head practically back-to-front.

They are contortionists, sometimes referred to as ''people without bones.'' But the key to their extraordinary elasticity really lies in the soft tissue that covers and links their bones. Called connective tissue, this includes the muscles, ligaments and tendons. From a very young age, contortionists practise hard at stretching their connective tissue until they can extend it beyond all normal limits.

The soft, connective parts of your body are like a series of interconnecting rubber bands. Your body has thousands of ''rubber bands'' in the form of muscles, tendons and ligaments. Every move you make involves many of these elastic bands joining together in a team effort, some of them relaxing, others being pulled tight.

Here's how you can feel this going on. Bend your upper arm as though you were ''making a muscle.'' Use your other hand to feel what happens when you do this. The biceps muscle in your upper arm actually tightens up, while the triceps muscle at the back of the arm relaxes. When straightening your arm, the biceps loosen while the triceps contract.

Athletes, particularly gymnasts and figure skaters, put extraordinary demands on their connective tissues. It takes super flexibility to execute a triple axel or perform a back walkover on a balance beam.

Watch the sidelines and you'll see athletes doing 10-15 minutes of simple stretching exercises before a competition. They're limbering up, so they'll have a full range of motion in each joint and won't risk pulling a muscle or a tendon.

The rubber bands in your body won't keep their stretchiness unless you exercise them. Through inactivity, they can grow too tight or too loose, and the results can be stiffness and clumsiness, aches and pains.

How good is your flexibility?

These tests should give you an answer:

Flex test No. 1

1. Stand and cross your legs with one leg in front of the other.
2. Bend slowly at the waist and try to touch the floor in front of your toes. *Don't bounce!*
3. Hold yourself in this position for about five seconds.

If you can do this, you have good flexibility in the muscles at the back of your thighs.

Flex test No. 2

1. Take off your shoes and stand on your heels with your toes lifted off the floor.
2. Walk straight ahead 10 steps.

If you can do this without losing your balance, you have good flexibility in your Achilles' tendons.

Flex test No. 3

1. Sit on a table top with your legs hanging over the edge and the backs of your knees touching the edge of the table. Separate your knees by several centimetres (a few inches).
2. Tuck in your chin and slowly bend forward. Try to lower your head all the way between your knees.

If you can do this, you have good flexibility in your lower back.

OKAY, so grown-ups are usually taller and stronger than kids. And they have more skill at sports. Not only that, they get to stay up later. But being young gives you an edge on a lot of things. Here are a couple of things you can take advantage of.

Flexibility Test
Challenge some grown-ups to this flexibility test. Who wins—them or you?

1. Sit on the floor with your legs sticking straight out in front of you.
2. Bend forward and touch your toes.
3. Now see how far past your toes you can reach. Have a friend measure the distance.

If you're under 12, you're probably more flexible than any of the adults. That's why the top female gymnasts are in their early teens or younger—they need that extra flexibility to perform the "pipe cleaner" bends required to win in competition. But don't gloat about your flexibility—once you reach puberty, you'll start to lose flexibility, too.

Boys will lose more flexibility than girls. Females have more of a hormone called relaxin, which softens and stretches their ligaments—pieces of tissue like strong elastic bands that connect bones to each other. Because women have more relaxin, their joints are more flexible and can bend farther than men's.

Centre of Gravity Test

Everyone's body has a centre of gravity, or balance point. Scientifically, the centre of gravity is the point in any object around which its weight is equally distributed. For example: Take a pen and place it across your finger so that it balances there perfectly. The point at which the pen stays without tipping is its centre of gravity.

The same goes for bodies (although they're harder to balance on your finger).

In this test the object is to touch the target on this page with your nose without losing your balance.

1. Put the book on the floor open to this page.
2. Kneel on the floor with your elbows against your knees and your fingertips touching the edge of the target.
3. Straighten up and put your hands behind your back.
4. Bend over and try touching the centre of the target with your nose.

Who's best at this test—girls, boys, women or men? Who's worst? Picking out the best group may be difficult. The worst group will be obvious.

You can do this test only if your centre of gravity remains in the area directly above your knees and feet. Men tend to have broader shoulders and more muscular chests and arms, while women have broader hips and more weight in the lower part of their bodies. This gives men a higher centre of gravity than women. When a man stretches forward, his high centre of gravity shifts outside the zone above his knees and feet, and he falls over. But because a woman's centre of gravity is lower, it remains within the balance zone, allowing her to reach the target without tipping over.

The closer your centre of gravity is to the ground, the more stable you are.

Why is it difficult to pick out a pattern in the test results of boys and girls? Because—until kids are in their teens—there's no difference in weight distribution. Until then, your results on this test are due to your own unique body.

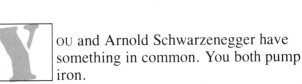

YOU and Arnold Schwarzenegger have something in common. You both pump iron.

That's right, the mineral iron is constantly being pumped through your arteries and veins, as it is through Arnold's. And the muscle that does all the pumping is the heart. Just like the biceps in your arms or the quadriceps in your legs, your heart is a muscle.

The heart is the body's strongest muscle. And no wonder. Every day, it flexes about 100 000 times, pumping 12 000 L (3 170 gallons) of blood. In one year, your heart pumps enough blood to fill a supertanker.

Pick up a tennis ball and squeeze it. The force that your hand uses to squeeze the ball is about equal to the force that it takes for your heart to pump iron (and all the other blood components) through your system.

Pumping greater amounts of weight with your arms makes your biceps grow bigger and stronger. The same thing happens to your heart. The more blood it pumps during a vigorous workout, the bigger and stronger it grows. Some athletes have hearts that can pump twice as much blood as an average person's heart.

A well-exercised heart also doesn't need to work as hard throughout the day because it can pump more blood with every beat. There are athletes in such good condition that their regular heartbeat is down around 40 beats per minute. When tennis champion Bjorn Borg was at the height of his career, he reportedly had a resting heart rate of 27 beats a minute. How fast does your heart beat?

Hear a Heartbeat

You'll need:
cardboard tube
a watch that shows seconds
a friend

1. Press one end of the cardboard tube against your friend's chest. Put your ear to the other end and listen to the constant rhythm—"lub, dub; lub, dub; lub, dub."

2. Time your friend's heart rate. Every "lub, dub" equals one beat. Count the number of beats in 10 seconds and then multiply by six. Girls and boys have a heart rate of about 80 beats a minute. Adults have a slightly slower rate—about 70 beats a minute. A baby's heart trips along at 130 times a minute. As you get older, and your metabolism slows down, your heart doesn't need to pump as quickly.

See a Heartbeat

You'll need:
a bathroom scale—not a digital one, but one with an arrow and a spinning dial

1. Do a couple of dozen jumping jacks to get your heart racing.
2. Step on the scale and look closely at the dial. What do you see?

The small vibrations of the needle are in time with your heart.

Your blood is pumping so hard through your body that it makes the scale shake.

Why does the heart speed up during exercise? Your circulating blood carries oxygen to your muscles and other parts of your body. Just as in an engine, your muscles need oxygen to help them burn fuel (fats and carbohydrates). Naturally, when your muscles work harder they require more oxygen, and the heart pumps faster to supply it.

At rest, only about 20 per cent of your blood is distributed to your muscles. During exercise, they receive about 80 per cent.

Calculate a Heartbeat

What's the fastest your heart can beat?

220 minus your age = your maximum heart rate
per minute

Any physical activity that pushes your heartbeat up to 70 per cent of its maximum rate, and keeps it there for 15 to 30 minutes, is good for your heart.

Animal	Heartbeats per minute
Shrew	1200
Canary	1000
Mouse	650
Porcupine	280
Golden Hamster	280
Chicken	200
Chihuahua	120
House cat	110
St. Bernard dog	80
Giraffe	60
Tasmanian Devil	54 - 66
Kangaroo	40 - 50
Tiger	40 - 50
Elephant	25
Beluga Whale	15 - 16
Gray Whale	8

TAKE A DEEP BREATH

ANT to get to know somebody better? Well, not just some body…your body. There are lots of things you know about yourself—how tall you are, what colour eyes you have, how far apart you can stretch your hands. Those are all parts of yourself that you can see. But what about the parts you can't see? Your lungs, for instance. How much air can they hold? Here's a way to find out.

Try Your Lungs on for Size

You'll need:
a big plastic bag (such as a kitchen garbage bag)
a marker that will write on the bag
a funnel
a container (such as a pitcher) marked off in litres
(quarts)

1. Bunch together the opening of the bag to make a mouthpiece, the way you would with a paper bag you were planning to blow up and burst. Make the mouth opening wide so you can breathe into the bag with your mouth open.
2. Squeeze the bag to get the air out.
3. Hold the bag away from your mouth and take two normal slow breaths.
4. On the next breath, breathe in as much air as you can, then bring the plastic bag to your mouth.

5. Pinch your nose and breathe out hard in one breath into the bag. Keep your mouth open—don't purse your lips as though you were blowing. Continue pushing the air out until you feel as though every last drop of air is squeezed from your lungs. (Hint: It helps to bend forward as you breathe out.)

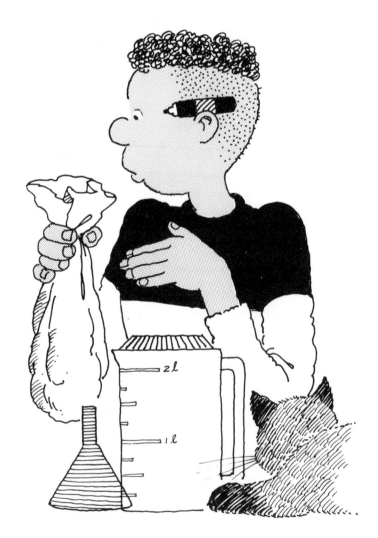

6. Close the bag tightly and hold it while you take it away from your mouth.
7. Slide your hand down the neck of the bag until the bag is completely expanded. Mark the bag at the point where you're holding it, in case your grip slips.

8. Push the neck of the funnel into the mouth of the bag, still keeping a firm hold on the bag so it doesn't move. Don't worry about the air escaping—you don't need it.

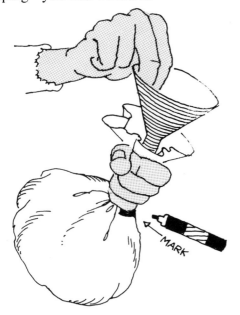

9. Using the marked container, carefully pour water into the bag until it's as fully expanded with water as it was with air. The bag will get quite heavy, so you may want to rest it on something as you fill it.

This will give you an approximate idea of your lung capacity.

The average 137 cm (4 foot 6 inch) tall boy has a lung capacity of approximately 2 L (2 quarts). The average 152 cm (5 foot) tall girl has a lung capacity of about 2.7 L (3 quarts). Compare your lung capacity to that of friends who are the same sex and height as you are.

F ind an empty space. Run. Which helps you move fast—your legs or your arms?

You may be surprised to learn that you need both. You run *on* your legs and *with* your arms.

Running or walking requires that the human body use its energy to move forward in a straight line, which is a lot trickier than you might think. Why tricky?

To find out, go for a stroll around the room. What does each arm do when the leg on the same side moves forward? What happens to your body if you hold your arms still?

Whenever you put a foot forward, you throw your body off balance. Swing your right foot forward, and your body automatically sways to the left. Swing your left foot forward, and your body sways to the right. Sway to the left, sway to the right, and you'll find yourself weaving down the road.

People use their arms to counterbalance their leg action. Every leg movement is matched by an equal and opposite arm movement, which acts to minimize side-to-side swaying. Thanks to your arm motion, you can walk in a straight line.

Try these goofy gaits

Here are some goofy gaits that mix up the natural leg-arm rhythm that keeps you moving straight ahead.

- Go for a walk, but reverse your regular arm motion. Whenever you swing your left leg forward, swing your left arm forward with it. Swing your right arm forward with your right leg. Keep this up as you move down the street. Don't be fazed when fellow pedestrians whisper, "Nerd."

- Walk at a regular pace but pump your arms back and forth twice as fast as you're moving your legs. You'll probably find that your legs will speed up to keep in time with your arms, proving once again the strong connnection between arm and leg action.

- Clasp your hands together and hold them against your chest. Run quickly. You'll probably find that your shoulders swing forward farther than they usually do, particularly as you go faster. Your shoulders are pinch-hitting for your absent arm motion.

- Get down on the carpet and do a goofy crawl. Put your right hand forward at the same time as you put your right knee forward. Now put your left hand and knee forward at the same time. Babies learn very early how to synchronize the movements of their arms and legs.

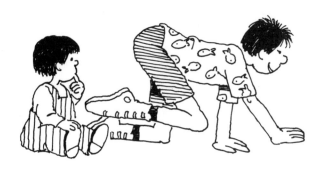

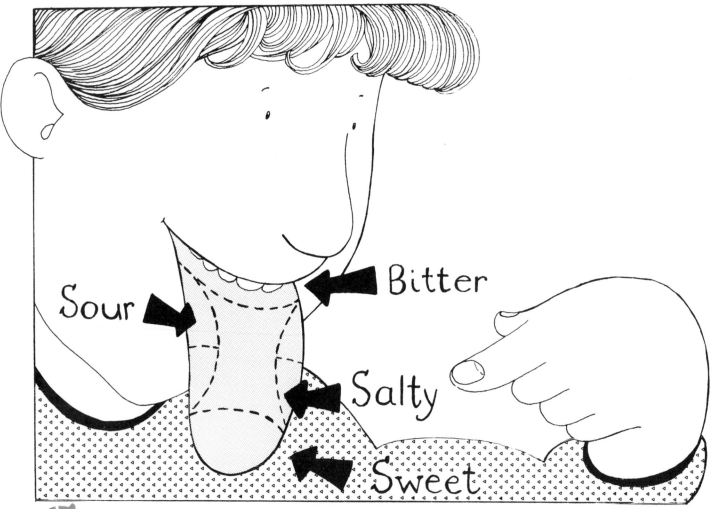

STICK your tongue out and look at it. Can you count the bumps on it? They're full of taste buds, about 9000 of them.

Taste buds helped warn primitive people whether the leaf or berry or bush they were eating was safe. If it tasted bad, it probably was bad, possibly poisonous, so they spit it out. Babies still do the same thing: they taste everything.

Today, you count on your taste buds to determine how good something is, not how safe it is. Your taste buds help you tell the difference between chocolate and vanilla, cheese and chicken—even Pepsi and Coke. And they do it all with just four tastes: bitter, sour, sweet and salt.

The smell, feel, texture and look of food also contributes to how good—or bad—it tastes. That's why food tastes so bland and boring when you have a cold. You can't smell it.

If you've ever had the bad luck to munch on a hot chili pepper, you'll know that you don't taste anything. Instead it feels as if your tongue is on fire. Spicy foods like curry or hot peppers create "heat" in your mouth by reacting with nerve endings on your tongue.

snacks are easiest to identify, even with your nose plugged?

Try the experiment again with a few changes. Keep the blindfold on, but don't hold your nose. Instead, rub a little vanilla extract or peanut butter or cinnamon on your upper lip. Do you think it will change the scores?

The tasty tongue

Place a little sugar on different parts of your tongue. When do you actually taste it? Do the same with lemon juice, salt, tonic water. Try other tastes too.

Try this experiment again after you've sucked on an ice cube for a minute or so. Does it make any difference?

The nose knows

Prepare a sample plate of bite-sized snacks, everything from carrots and radishes to bologna and chocolate. Then, with friends, take turns tasting them while you wear a blindfold and hold your nose so you can neither see nor smell what you are eating. Try and figure out what you are actually tasting. Keep score to see which of you has the best sense of taste. Which

Eye see how good it is

Ask your parents if you can fix an experimental rainbow meal. Use a little food colouring to create blue milk, green gravy, red mashed potatoes, etc. You can even put celery in a glass of water with food colouring in it to change it as well. Who in the family eats it? Did they feel it changed the taste of the food to have it presented in living colour?

OPEN WIDE

FIND a mirror and open wide. Your mouthful of pearly whites are precision tools you probably take for granted. Each kind of tooth is well suited to the job it has to do.

Your incisors and cuspids have single roots and single cutting edges for biting and tearing through foods.

Your bicuspids and molars have two or more roots. They have broad, chewing, grinding surfaces for chewing and crushing food to aid digestion.

Did you know?
- Prehistoric children didn't eat refined sugars so they had almost no tooth decay.
- According to *The Guinness Book of World Records*, the strongest teeth in the world belong to a Belgian man named John "Hercules" Passis. In 1977 he raised a 233 kg (513 pound) weight 15 cm (6 inches) off the ground with his teeth. Two years later, he kept a helicopter from taking off using a mouth harness.
- Your teeth wear down more as you get older and the amount they wear down depends on your diet. Primitive people's teeth showed more wear because they ate rough food. Today, your food is softer, so your teeth wear down less.
- People don't chew up and down. They chew side to side, something like cows do.
- The people with the largest teeth are the Inuit and Australian Aborigines. The smallest teeth belong to African Bushmen and Laplanders.
- According to *The Guinness Book of World Records*, the most valuable tooth belonged to Sir Isaac Newton. It was bought for $1300 in 1816 by a nobleman who wore it in a ring.

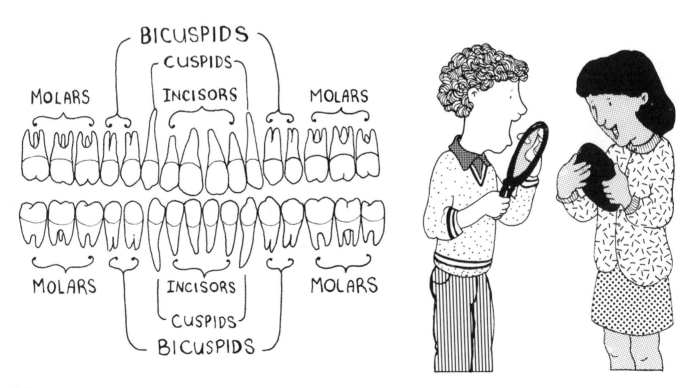

Some snacks that are bad for your teeth	
cake, cookies, donuts	figs
candy	raisins
ice cream	grapes
apple juice	gum
cocoa	marshmallows
soft drinks, sweetened juices	peanut butter
dates	jam or jelly

Some snacks that are good for your teeth	
nuts	corn chips
popcorn (plain)	cheese
carrots	oranges
celery	tomatoes
potato chips	milk
olives	

Bite with your chewers

See if you can make your teeth do a different job than they were made for. Bite into an apple with your molars and chew it with your incisors and cuspids.

The acid test

Plaque is bacteria on your teeth. It feeds on sugar and gives off an acid as waste. The acid is what makes holes or cavities in your teeth. To see how easily acid can eat through teeth, place pieces of eggshell in two cups. Like teeth, eggshell is mostly made of calcium. Cover the eggshell in one cup with a bit of water and cover the other with vinegar, which is an acid. Leave the eggshells until all the water and vinegar evaporate. What condition are they in? Is there anything left in the cup?

Green teeth?

Your dentist has probably stained your teeth red to show where you missed brushing. You can do the same thing at home by brushing and then swishing food colouring around in your mouth (but don't swallow it!). The colour sticks best to plaque, so it's darker where you missed brushing. If you want to look really frightening, the splotchy unbrushed look is great—especially for Hallowe'en! (Your tongue may turn colour too, but it washes off fairly easily.)

SWALLOW THIS

URE, you've travelled before—to school or maybe to the other side of the world. But have you ever travelled down a human throat?

Imagine you're a hamburger. Just what happens after you and your buns get bitten?

First, you get chewed. Spit, or saliva, has a special chemical called an enzyme which starts digesting food as it's chewed.

Getting down a throat, or esophagus, is not a simple matter. As you start off, a small flap of tissue called the epiglottis closes over the entrance to the windpipe. Let's face it. You may be a great-tasting hamburger, but no body wants you in its lungs.

Next, you get some heavy duty bear hugs from muscles in the esophagus. They don't believe you can find your way to the stomach unless they push you there. These waves of pushing are called peristalsis.

Finally, you get a little elbow room. You slide into the stomach and it shuts behind you. You can't get out of this 1L (1 quart) pouch. You're churned around like clothes in a washing machine. The stomach muscles also think squeezing is just what a hamburger needs. You meet up with more enzymes and a liquid called hydrochloric acid. These break you down into even smaller bits.

After a couple of hours, you look like a real mess—more soup than hamburger. Then the stomach opens up an exit and you're glad to be on your way.

Not so fast. The trip isn't over yet. You're being squeezed into the small intestine—and it's not that small. It must be 6 or 7 m (20 or 22 feet) long in here! More chemicals are dumped on you to help digestion along, first enzymes from the pancreas and then bile from the liver.

Finally the body decides you're ready to be used. Protein, glucose, fats and water are pulled out of you by lots of folds in the small intestine that look like fingers sticking out. These "villi" are just waiting to sop up all your nutrients and pass them along to the bloodstream.

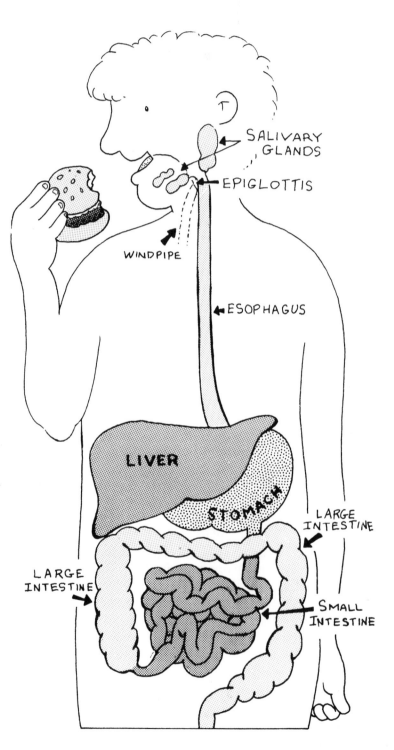

The small intestine has a motto: "If you can't use it, eliminate it." But it's the large intestine that handles the waste disposal job. It's wider than the small intestine and only about 1 m (3 feet) long. It's got a heavy duty job to do. It finishes soaking up water and minerals. Then it collects what's left of you—the waste products that the body can't use—and pushes them out, along with a lot of dead bacteria, in the form of feces or stool.

What an exciting journey for a hamburger to take—and you didn't even need a ticket.

Digestion in space
Even though digestion is helped by gravity, there's no problem eating in space where there is no gravity. Muscle movement, or peristalsis, still gets food where it needs to go.

Spit on it
To see how the digestion process works, try this experiment. Take a small piece of meat and put it in a tiny container. Put enough of your saliva in with it to cover the meat. Let it stand for a day. What do you see?

A window to the stomach
A French Canadian, Alexis St. Martin, was accidentally shot in his side on June 6, 1822. Dr. Beaumont treated him, and although St. Martin recovered, he had an opening nearly 2 cm (¾ inch) across that led directly into his stomach. Dr. Beaumont used him as human guinea pig to study how the stomach actually works. St. Martin lived with the hole in his stomach until he died in 1880, at the age of 82.

Dr. William Beaumont *examining the hole in Alexis St. Martin's stomach.*

THINGS THAT GO GROWL IN THE STOMACH

A BURP is just a bit of wind
Forced upward from the chest.
But when it takes a downward path,
It's then called flatulence.

But what makes that wind?
You may well ask,
'Tis a question most perplexing.

It's the foods you eat
And stuff you drink
Being mushed up in digesting.

And as it's dissolved
By stomach walls
You can hear the food a-churning.

But at other times
Your stomach growls:
"It's food for which I'm a-yearning."

Your burps and flatulence are caused by trapped air
and gas. Stomach growls, called borborygmus, are
made by your intestines contracting. The louder the
sounds, the harder they're working.

Everyone is different, especially when it comes to
burps, flatulence and growls. A meal that will turn a
friend's stomach into a rock and roll band might
leave yours as quiet as a turned-off radio.

Stomach turn-ons

Find out what turns a stomach on. Put your ear
against a friend's stomach before a meal. What do
you hear? Record your observations in detail and
then listen again after trying some of the foods below.
Is there any difference in sound? Does your friend
have more flatulence after some foods than others?

onions	peanuts	melons
raw apples	cooked cabbage	chocolate
baked beans	radishes	lettuce
milk	cucumbers	eggs
cauliflower		

Bigger and better burps

Burps are just your body's way of getting rid of excess
gas. Can you make bigger burps by increasing the
amount of gas in your stomach? Try chewing gum,
gulping down air or a carbonated beverage.

Pick a cure—any cure

Have you ever had the hiccoughs so long you thought you'd never talk again without sounding like a broken record? One man, Charles Osborne, started hiccoughing in 1922 and is still going. Although he says he's had a normal life, including being married and having eight children, he can't keep his false teeth in.

What causes hiccoughs? Lots of things, ranging from getting upset to eating a meal that's too spicy. Whatever the cause, the result is the same. Your diaphragm, a large muscle across your chest which moves up and down when you breathe, starts contracting in jerks. To stop your hiccoughs, all you have to do is shock your diaphragm out of its contractions.

There are lots of cures for hiccoughs, and every single one of them works—sometimes. Next time you start hiccoughing try one of these diaphragm shockers:

- a good fright
- eating a spoonful of crushed ice
- pressing in just a little bit on your closed eyeballs
- swallowing a large spoonful of dried breadcrumbs
- gulping a tablespoon of peanut butter
- eating a spoonful of sugar
- sucking on a lemon
- drinking a large glass of water in one gulp
- holding your breath
- standing on your head and breathing through your nose.

THAT SINKING FEELING

I F you think of food as packages of vitamins, proteins and nutrients, think of fibre as the string that holds all those packages together.

Fibre, also called roughage, is really non-food food—it's food that your stomach can't digest. You get it from whole grain breads and cereals, fruits and vegetables and legumes (dried beans and peas).

If you don't digest it, why eat it? Because you still use it. Fibre passes through your body quickly and acts like a neighbourhood garbage truck. It picks up waste in your intestines and carries it out through your bowels.

Get enough fibre and going to the bathroom is a lot easier. Fibre adds bulk to your stool. It also holds water. People who get plenty of fibre in their diets produce floaters. Their stool is big, soft and bulky and passes quickly. But if you don't eat enough fibre you produce sinkers—small, hard stools that are difficult and, at times, even painful to pass.

Nutritionists recommend you get between 28 and 40 g (1–1½ ounces) of fibre a day. A balanced diet including wide selection from all the food groups (dairy, meat, vegetable and fruit, bread and cereal) is the best way to guarantee your body gets what it needs.

Fibre test

Can you guess which foods in this list have the most fibre and which ones have the least? Number them from 1 to 8. Number 1 is the food with the most fibre; number 8 is the food with the least fibre. (Answers on page 188.)

1 slice whole-wheat bread
1 slice white bread
1 apple
16 grapes
1 egg
1 raw carrot
2 shredded wheat biscuits
125 mL (½ cup) baked beans

TALE OF TWO RATS

WHAT would you look like if you ate all the junk food you wanted? Probably a lot like Leon the rat.

Leon and his friend Harry grew up together. There the similarities ended.

Leon was raised in what seemed like paradise. Fat was mixed with his regular food so that his diet was like a human's who eats lots of french fries, fried chicken and other fried food. He had all the "goodies" anyone could want—sweetened milk and water, hot dogs, snacks of cookies, chocolate bars and potato chips.

Leon never exercised, either. He spent all his free time waiting around his cage for yet another yummy handout.

The result? Leon was one fat rat.

Old buddy Harry was another story entirely. Harry only chowed down on nutritious food with little fat. What's more, he drank only water. His favourite pastime was putting in a few laps on his exercise wheel.

He was one rat in tip top shape.

Besides being too fat to do much or enjoy life, Leon was eating foods that were dangerous for him—the same way that diets like his are dangerous for humans. Eating lots of fat and food with little nutrition in it can lead to big health problems, including heart disease.

Like rats, you need a balanced diet. Junk food may sound pretty good but what your body really craves is not just another potato chip but selections from the four food groups: dairy, fruits and vegetables, grains and meat. You need them all for your body to grow strong and healthy. Exercise helps to keep it that way.

Just like Harry the rat.

ASK DOCTOR FOOD

DEAR **Dr. Food:** *Why do I sometimes feel hungry?*
When your stomach is empty, it starts to contract. It starts with a rhythm of about three contractions per minute but soon they happen more often, last longer and are stronger. This sends a message to your brain: "Send food down here. Fast!"

Dear Dr. Food: *If I didn't have a stomach would I still get hungry?*
Strangely enough, yes, you would! People who have had their stomachs surgically removed still feel hungry at times. Why? Your stomach works together with a part of your brain called the appestat to tell you you've got that empty feeling. Even without your stomach's help, the appestat still works. Part of the appestat tells you: "Start eating, you're hungry." When you've had enough to eat, another part of the appestat says, "Stop now, you're full."

No one is really sure how the appestat works. It might be like the thermostat in your house, which tells your furnace to turn on the heat because the house is getting cold and then shuts the furnace off when it's warm enough. Your appestat might turn your hunger on—telling your body it needs to burn fuel to keep you going—when the temperature of your blood goes down slightly. When the temperature goes up, it shuts off.

Your appestat might also work as a sensor. When there's not enough glucose (a form of sugar) in your blood, it shouts, "CHOW TIME!"

Dear Doctor Food: *Sometimes after I've eaten, I feel like the food is sitting in my stomach like a rock.*
The way you eat and digest food is often affected by the way you feel. Were you upset or angry when you got that rock-in-the-stomach feeling?

Scientists discovered that how we feel affects our digestion by observing a man named Tom. Tom couldn't swallow food because his esophagus, the

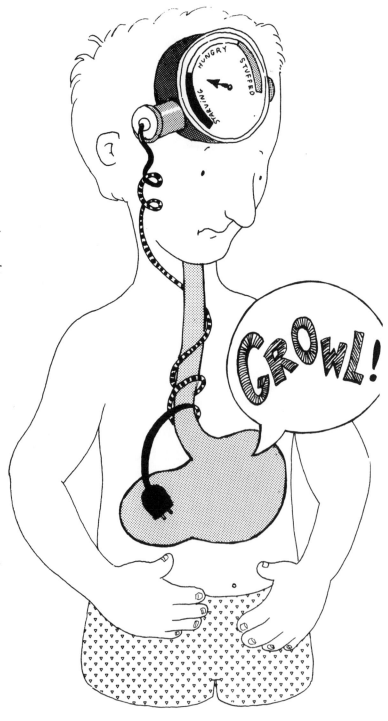

tube through which food passes on its way to the stomach, was damaged. He learned how to chew his food and then take it out of his mouth and put it in a special rubber tube that went directly into his stomach.

Tom lived like this for years, and one day he agreed to be part of a study. Two doctors looked through the tube into his stomach and watched what happened every time Tom ate.

When Tom got mad, the doctors noticed that his stomach lining changed from pink to bright red and his stomach juices flowed more quickly. If he then ate a meal, the food passed through his stomach even faster than it usually would.

When Tom was unhappy, afraid or depressed, his stomach also changed colours, but instead of bright red, it turned very pale. There were also fewer stomach juices. Even when Tom ate, the normal amount of digestive juices weren't there and his food just sat there for hours, undigested.

So the next time you sit down to eat—whether it's peanut butter or stewed liver in spinach sauce—remember that how you feel may affect your meal as much as how you feel about the meal itself.

Appetite tester

What turns your appetite on? Think of a lemon. Does it make you feel hungry? Now think of chocolate cake. How do you feel? Do you notice any changes in your stomach or your mouth? Do you react differently when you do this experiment right after a big meal?

47

YOU ARE THE FOOD

YOU don't feel it, you don't even notice it, but you're being eaten, little by little, right now! And you can't even see most of the creatures that are munching on you.

No matter how much soap you use, you always have bacteria on you and in you. In fact, you have more microbes—microscopic organisms such as bacteria, yeast and viruses—on and in your body than there are people on the entire Earth! You have them on your skin and hair, inside your nose, mouth and in your intestines. And you provide their breakfast, lunch and dinner.

To give you an idea of their size, it would take 9 trillion medium-sized bacteria to fill a box the size of a package of chewing gum sticks. There are about 300 000 of these tiny microbes on any dime-sized section of your skin.

Fortunately, most of the bacteria in your body are not only necessary, they're friendly. The microbes on your skin, for instance, are scavengers. They look for other bacteria to eat and feed on your dead skin cells.

The bacteria in your intestines, called Escherichia coli, or E. coli for short, eat some of the leftover fibre that your body can't digest. As they eat, they break the fibre down and make its nutrients available to you. At the same time, they produce vitamin K and vitamin B12. Vitamin K helps your blood clot when you cut yourself, and vitamin B12 protects you from anemia, a sickness that makes you very run down and tired.

Although keeping yourself clean is important, scientists have discovered there's such a thing as getting rid of too many germs. They've raised super clean animals; animals that are totally microbe free. Rather than being healthier, these animals get sick more easily! Without the microbes that should be in their bodies, the animals have trouble fighting off the germs that don't belong. Microbe-free animals also have weaker hearts and their intestines don't work the way they should.

So not only do you have to feed your body to stay healthy, you have to feed your body's bacteria. Some things you eat, like yogurt and cheese, contain bacteria that are good for you because they build up the bacteria in your body.

You're eaten not only by things you can't see but by things you *can* see—like mosquitos and black flies. Although you look at them as pests, they look at your blood as a meal. Without you and other animals to snack on, their lives just wouldn't be liveable.

So next time someone asks, "What's eating you?"—tell them.

What you can't do

There is no simple, safe way for you to see the microbes that live on you. You could see them individually with a powerful light microscope or an electron microscope or in numbers by growing them in a sterile nutrient solution, but those methods require specialized equipment. However there is a way for you to see another kind of microscopic organism.

What you can do: grow mould

You'll need:

a clean pie plate
a piece of paper towel
a piece of bread (white bread is easiest to observe
  but takes longer)
plastic wrap

1. Wet the paper towel and lay it on the pie plate.
2. Place the slice of bread on it.
3. Cover it all with plastic wrap and put in in a dark place.
4. Leave it for a few days, then look at it. Try looking at it through a magnifying glass or with a microscope, if you have one. You're seeing clusters of tiny microscopic organisms called moulds. Moulds are a different kind of organism from the ones that live on you; they're more plant than animal. But like your body microbes, moulds are so small that you can't see them, even though they're in the air and on surfaces all around you. When they find a suitable environment such as some nice damp bread, they grow in great numbers and become visible.

FOOL YOURSELF (OR A FRIEND)

CHALLENGE your friends. Ask them to make a hole in a piece of notebook paper big enough to pass their whole body through without ripping the paper. Sound impossible? Here's how to do it.

You'll need:
a piece of paper (almost any size writing paper will do)
scissors

1. Fold the paper so that the two short ends meet.
2. Cut out a rectangle along the fold, as shown.
3. Make 13 cuts in the paper, as shown in the diagram.
4. Carefully stretch the paper out and you'll be able to climb through the hole. If the hole is a tight squeeze, try again on another piece of paper. This time, make more cuts. There must always be an odd number of cuts and they must follow the pattern.
5. Try it on a smaller piece of paper. How small can the paper be and still work?

How does it work?
What you've done is make it possible for the paper to stretch. If you carefully unfold the paper after you make the cuts and examine it, you'll see that there are points where the paper is strongly held together and other areas where it can pull away from the neighbouring section. In a way, this is how the molecules of rubber alter their shape when you stretch them.

an odd number of cuts.

MOEBIUS STRIP

 OU'VE probably heard the expression, "There are two sides to everything." But are there? You can find out.

You'll need:
several strips of paper about 25 cm (10 inches) long and about 2 cm (1 inch) wide
tape
scissors
2 different coloured crayons or felt markers

1. Make a circle out of one of the strips of paper and tape the ends together. Cut it in half around the middle. What do you get? Surprised? No, of course not.
2. Take another strip of paper. But this time, make a half-twist in it before you tape the ends together. Now cut this one in half down the middle. Oops! What happened?
3. Find out by making two more circles of paper, one with a half-twist and one without.
4. Test them with the crayons. Start with the plain strip. Put one crayon on the outside and trace it around until you come back to the beginning. Now put your other crayon on the unmarked side and draw a line until you come back to the beginning. Two sides, two colours, right? Now try the same thing with your twisted strip.
5. Try another test. Colour one edge of your plain circle. Try colouring one edge of the twisted one.

What's going on?
The circle with the half-twist is the amazing one-sided, one-edged Moebius strip, named after Ferdinand Moebius, the mathematician who discovered it. It behaves in some surprising, but consistent, ways. When you cut your two-sided, two-edged strip in half, you get two pieces, with a total of four edges and four sides. Your cut-in-half Moebius strip is still in one piece, but how many edges and sides does it have?

If you cut an ordinary strip of paper around the middle twice, you'll end up with three separate pieces, with a total of six edges and six sides. Try cutting your Moebius strip around the middle twice. Surprised? See if you can guess how many sides and edges you have before checking them out.

Next time someone's cooking with eggs around your house, save the eggshells so that you can astound your friends with this incredible stunt.

You'll need:
4 raw eggs
a small pair of scissors
masking tape
some books that are all about the same size

1. To crack the eggs and get four empty eggshells, gently break open the small end of each egg by tapping it on a table or counter.
2. Carefully peel away some of the eggshell.
3. Pour or scoop out the egg inside.
4. Put a piece of masking tape around the middle of each eggshell. This will prevent the eggshell from cracking when you cut it.
5. Carefully cut around the eggshell, through the masking tape, so that you have four half-eggshells with even bottoms.
6. Put the eggshells on a table, open end down, in a rectangle that's just a bit smaller than one of your books.
7. Lay a book on the eggshells. Do any of the shells crack?
8. Keep adding books until — CRRRACKK! How many books can you stack on the eggs? (For a real eye opener, weigh the books and see how many kilograms it took to break the shells.)

Why does it happen?
Each half of the eggshell is a miniature dome, and domes are one of the strongest shapes. Why? Weight on the top of the dome is carried down along the curved walls to the wide base. No single point on the dome supports the whole weight of the object on top of it. That's why domes are often used for big buildings that can't have pillar supports, such as hockey rinks and arenas.

Eggshell Trivia
Staff at the Ontario Science Centre in Toronto have shown that a single egg can support a 90 k (200 pound) person.

STRONGMAN'S SECRET

AN you pull two broomsticks together — even if your strongest friends are trying to hold them apart?

You'll need:
2 brooms
a strong rope or piece of clothesline at least 3 m (9 feet) long

1. Ask two friends to hold the broomsticks about 30 cm (1 foot) apart, and challenge a strong friend to pull them together. When your strong friend has admitted defeat, you try it.
2. Tie one end of the rope securely around one broomstick.
3. Wind the rope around the two broomsticks, as shown.
4. Pull the free end of the rope. Presto! No matter how hard your two friends resist the pull, you can easily draw the broomsticks together.

How does it work?
By winding the rope around the broomsticks as you did, you used technology. Technology is the use of tools, materials, machines, and techniques to make work easier. In this case, wrapping the rope increases your pulling power. In fact, every turn of the rope approximately *doubles* your pulling power. But there's a hitch. Every time you double your pulling power, you must pull the free end of the rope twice as far.

This system of using a rope to increase your strength is a simple block and tackle. You can see the block and tackle being used on construction sites to lift heavy loads, in loading ships, and for lowering pianos from buildings. Remember, when Superman isn't available, technology is!

Ave you ever seen a magician whip a tablecloth out from under a full setting of dishes without even rattling a glass? There's no magic involved — only the clever use of science.

We don't recommend that you use dinner dishes for this. Instead, here's a safer — and cheaper — version of the tablecloth trick that will astound your family.

You'll need:
a heavy water glass
a strip of newspaper long enough to reach over the rim of the glass and hang over the edges
2 pennies
a ruler

1. Put one end of the strip of paper over the rim of the glass, as pictured.
2. Balance the two pennies on top of the paper, on the rim of the glass. Make sure the pennies are balanced on the rim and are not supported by the paper.

3. Lift the free end of the paper so that it is horizontal. Be careful not to move the coins.
4. Strike the paper with a ruler about 4 cm (1 ½ inches) from the edge of the glass. Speed is important. It might take a few tries before you get the hang of it, but before long, you should be able to whip the paper out from under the coins, leaving them balanced on the edge of the glass.

How does it work?

Inertia is a property of all things that makes them resist any change in their motion. When an object is standing still, it takes a force to get it moving. And once it is moving, it takes a force to stop it.

The heavier an object is, the more force — or time — it takes to change its momentum. That's the key to doing this trick. You can change the momentum of one part, the light paper, without changing the momentum of the other, the heavy pennies.

MYSTERIOUS BREAKING STRING

ERE'S another inertia trick that will puzzle your friends.

You'll need:

a medium-sized hardcover book

2 kinds of string, one stronger than the other, but both should break when you tug them. The weaker piece should be long enough to tie around the book at least three times.

1. Tie the strong string firmly around the middle of the book.
2. Cut the weaker string into three pieces, each long enough to tie around the book.
3. Tie one piece of weak string to the strong string on top of the book and another piece to the bottom, as shown.
4. Hold the book by the top string and pull down steadily and hard on the bottom string. (You might need to wear a glove to protect your top hand.) If you keep pulling steadily, the top string will break.
5. Replace the broken string with the third piece of weak string.
6. Hold the book in the air as before, and give a short sharp pull on the bottom string. Now it's the bottom string that breaks. Why?

How does it work?

When you pull slowly and steadily on the bottom string, you gradually pull the book down. This stretches the top string. Since the top string is bearing both the weight of the book and the strength of your pull, it eventually breaks.

When you pull suddenly and sharply, something very different happens. What makes the difference is the inertia of the book. Inertia is the tendency of all objects to stay at rest until some outside force makes them move. The bottom string breaks before the force of your pull can overcome the book's inertia. Since the

weak string

strong string

weak string

book doesn't move, no extra force is placed on the top string, so it continues to hold.

If you hold the top string with your bare hand while you do these experiments, you'll feel the difference in the force that comes through to the top string — but it may pinch a bit!

57

RY balancing a ruler on one finger. To do it, you have to rest the midpoint of the ruler on your finger. Here's a ruler balancing trick that seems to defy the laws of gravity.

You'll need:
a piece of string
a ruler
a hammer, preferably rubber-handled

1. Tie the string in a loop and slip it over the ruler and the handle of the hammer.
2. As shown in the illustration, position the hammer and ruler with the end of the hammer resting against the ruler. Your friends won't believe that the ruler can balance when only the tip of it is on the table.

How does it work?
All objects have an imaginary spot called a centre of gravity that acts as if all the weight of the object were balanced there. The centre of gravity of a ruler is usually right in the middle of the ruler. But when you hang the heavy hammer from the ruler, you create a new system that has its centre of gravity near the head of the hammer so the ruler can balance from its tip.

Teeter-Totter Tip
If you've ever been on a teeter-totter with someone bigger than you, you know you're going to stay up in the air. The teeter-totter's pivot is right in the middle of the board you're sitting on, but there's more weight on one side of the board (your larger friend), than on the other (you). To get the teeter-totter balanced properly, you have to adjust the weights along the board so that the centre of gravity falls over the teeter-totter's pivot. The easiest way to do that is get your large friend to move towards you.

I F you put a tub of water on a scale and sat down in it, your weight would be added to the weight of the tub of water. But what if you just stuck your foot in the water without touching the bottom or sides of the tub? Would the scale register any added weight? Here's an experiment to help you solve this mystery.

You'll need:
2 water glasses, plastic are best
a strong ruler
a round pencil or a round dowel, the length of a pencil
tape

1. Tape the pencil or dowel to a table so it won't roll.
2. Balance the ruler across the pencil.
3. Put a glass on each end of the ruler. Pour water into each glass until they're about three-quarters full. Then adjust the amount of water in each glass until they balance evenly.
4. Stick your finger into the water in one of the glasses. Be sure you don't touch the bottom or sides of the glass. What happens to the balance? Try putting your finger into the other glass and see if the same thing happens.

How does it work?
How can your finger make the glass of water heavier when you're not touching the glass? Try it again, and this time watch what happens to the level of the water in the glass when you put your finger in.

Your finger has taken the place of some of the water, and the displaced water piles up above its former level. If the displaced water just disappeared, the weight of the glass — with your finger in it — wouldn't change. Your finger not only takes the space of some of the water, it also "fills in" for the weight of that water. But, since the displaced water is still there, the glass weighs more, by the same amount as the weight of that displaced water.

Would it make a difference if you held a finger-sized piece of metal in the water? How about a finger-sized piece of wood?

OUR friends will think you're using a magic ruler for this trick. No matter how out of balance it looks, the ruler won't fall.

You'll need:
a metre (yard)-long ruler

1. Ask a friend to hold his hands about 60 cm (2 feet) apart with his palms turned inwards.
2. Place the ruler on top of his hands so that one end of the stick is very close to one hand and the other end is sticking out past the other hand.
3. Challenge him to move his hands together until the ruler becomes imbalanced and falls. No matter how many times he tries it, the ruler won't fall.
4. Ask him to bring his hands together at a point other than the centre. Can he do it?

How does it work?
Friction keeps the ruler from falling. What is friction? All objects resist moving across one another, and this is called friction. The heavier the weight of the object on top, the greater the friction between it and the object it's resting on. The stick is heavier at the long end so there is more friction between it and the hand on that side, making it harder for the hand under the long end to slide. While that hand is prevented from sliding quickly, the other hand slides to meet it. Like magic, the ruler stays balanced, and your hands always meet at the centre.

 ERE are two optical illusions guaranteed to fool you.

Illusion #1
Are those stairs on the floor or the ceiling? Are your eyes fooling you? No . . . your brain is.

How does it work?
Just as you had to learn to read — to make sense out of squiggles on paper — so you had to learn to see — to make sense out of rays of light hitting your eyes. Once your brain has learned the "rules" of seeing (for example, the farther things are from you, the smaller they look), it applies those rules to interpret everything you look at. But when an object or a drawing breaks the rules, or when it could be interpreted in different ways, your brain may give you wrong or confusing information, and that's what we call an optical illusion.

As you look at the staircase, you'll see it seem to flip upside down. The back wall becomes the front wall, and the stairs hang from the ceiling. That's because the drawing contains equal information for both interpretations, so your brain can't decide which way is correct. It keeps switching back and forth in the way it interprets the picture.

Illusion #2
Here's an illusion you can make for yourself.

You'll need:
a piece of stiff paper
a table

1. Fold the paper in half. Make the fold sharp by running your fingernail along it.
2. Set it on the table as shown, cover one eye, and stare at the folded edge. What happens?

How does it work?
By placing the paper in an open space and by covering one eye, you make it very difficult to judge depth correctly. Your brain becomes confused about which way the paper is folded, and tries different ways of seeing it.

CAN you hold up 45 kg (100 pounds) on one hand? It's easy. Just hold out your hand, palm up. There, you've done it. That's the weight of air. Here's a heavy air trick to play on your friends.

You'll need:
a sheet of newspaper
a strong ruler

1. Put the ruler on a table with one end over the edge.
2. Fold the piece of newspaper along its fold and cover the portion of the ruler on the table with the newspaper, as shown.
3. Tell your friend you're going to put a spell on the paper so you won't be able to lift it. As if performing magic, wave your hand over the paper, then bring your fist down sharply on the free end of the ruler.

4. Then have your friend try hitting the free end of the ruler. The paper still won't lift. In fact, if either of you hit the ruler too hard, it could break, and the paper wouldn't even be torn.

How does it work?
The weight of the air pressing down on the newspaper resists being squeezed up suddenly and holds the ruler to the table. The pressure of air is about 103 kPa (15 pounds on every square inch). It's hard to believe that air is that heavy!

A ⌐⌐⌐ ⌐⌐ the bottom of an ocean of air ⌐⌐⌐ about 500 ⌐⌐ high! All ⌐⌐ presses down on us and everything around us. The reason we ⌐⌐ not crushed from the great pressure of all that air is that there's also air inside us and under us that's pressing outwards and upwards with the same pressure. So it equals out. Here are two experiments that let you see that air pressure exists.

Air Presses Up

You'll need:
an ordinary water glass
a piece of stiff, flat cardboard

1. Fill the glass with water right to the top.
2. Slide a piece of cardboard over the top of the glass, making sure no bubbles of air are left in the glass.
3. Hold the cardboard tight against the glass and turn the glass upside down over the sink. Take your hand away from the cardboard. What happens?

How does it work?

What keeps the cardboard in place is the pressure of the air pushing up from the outside. This air pressure is greater than the weight of the water pushing down on the cardboard from inside. As long as the cardboard does not get soggy and sag, it will stay in place by itself. If the cardboard was not firm and flat to begin with, it will let air in and water out, so this experiment won't work.

Blowing Air Away

You'll need:
2 long strips of paper, any size

1. Holding the two strips of paper a few centimetres (about 2 inches) apart, dangle them in front of you.
2. What do you think will happen if you blow steadily between the strips? They'll be blown apart, right?

How does it work?

Why do the strips move *together* when you blow between them, instead of *apart*? You're blowing the air away from between them and lowering the air pressure. The pressure of the air outside the strips becomes greater than the air between the strips, so the pieces of paper are pushed together.

AIR

NEXT time you're looking for an empty glass, we guarantee you won't be able to find one. Why? All glasses, even the ones that look empty, are full of air. You can prove that air takes up space — and amaze your friends — with this easy trick.

You'll need:
a glass
a paper towel

1. Tell your friends that you are going to put the paper towel in the glass and then plunge the glass into the sink without getting so much as a drop of water on the paper towel.
2. Here's how to do it. Stuff the paper towel into the bottom of the glass. Make sure it's in there securely so it won't fall out when you turn the glass upside down.
3. Fill a sink with water. Hold the glass straight upside down and plunge it into the water.
4. Count slowly to 10, then carefully lift the glass out of the sink. Make sure you keep it perfectly straight at all times. Your friends will hardly believe their eyes when you pull a dry paper towel out of the glass.

How does it work?
Water could not get into the glass because it was full of air. And the air could not get out because it is lighter than water and couldn't escape under the rim of the glass.

paper towel — glass

 OOL your friends with this clever balloon trick. It looks like a snap — but it's not!

You'll need:
a balloon
a pop bottle

1. Push the deflated balloon into the bottle and stretch the open end of the balloon back over the bottle's mouth.
2. Challenge a friend to blow up the balloon. No matter how hard he huffs and puffs, he won't be able to do it.

How does it work?
As you inflate the balloon, it takes up more space in the bottle. But the bottle is already full — of air. Even though you can't see it, air takes up space. When you try to inflate the balloon, the air trapped inside the bottle prevents you from doing it.

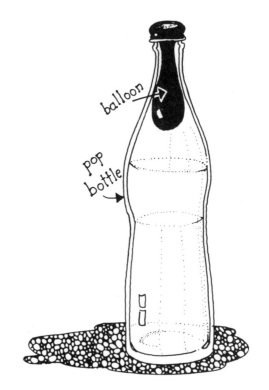

balloon

pop bottle

WATER PRESSURE PUZZLE 1

IF your fish tank sprung a leak, would the water spurt farther if the leak were nearer the top or the bottom of the tank? Here's how to find out.

You'll need:
an empty milk carton
a pen or pencil
a piece of adhesive tape the length of the carton

1. Use the pencil to punch three or four holes, one above the other, on one side of the carton. Make the top hole at least 3 cm (1 ¼ inches) from the top of the carton.
2. Cover the holes with the adhesive tape.
3. Fill the carton with water.
4. Hold the carton above a sink or bathtub. Strip off the tape quickly. Which stream of water travels farthest?

How does it work?
Water pressure and time are the keys to the answer. The water near the bottom of the carton has the force of all the water above it pushing it out, so the water coming from the bottom hole will go farthest.

I F the *depth* of the water makes the pressure greater, what about the amount of water?

You'll need:
a small, frozen juice can
a large coffee tin or litre (quart) size tin
adhesive tape
an awl, or other instrument for making a hole in tin

1. Punch a hole 2-3 cm (about one inch) from the bottom of each can.
2. Cover the holes with a strip of tape.
3. Fill each can with water to the same depth (e.g. 5 cm [2 inches] deep in each can). The larger can will take much more water to fill the same depth as the small can.
4. Hold both cans above a sink or bathtub. Get a friend to pull off the tape at the same time. Which stream goes farther?

WHY is a full glass of water like a bus at rush hour? Because you can usually put more into it! Surprise yourself by finding out how much more you can put into a full glass of water.

You'll need:
a glass
some food colouring
some coins

1. Fill a glass right to the top with water coloured with a few drops of food colouring.
2. Start gently dropping coins into the water. (It's best to hold the coins on edge and slip them into the water.) You'll notice that the top of the water bulges out above the top of the glass. How many coins can you add before the water overflows?

How does it work?
Water molecules have a strong attraction for one another. Inside the glass, the molecules that are surrounded by other molecules are attracted in all directions. But the molecules at the surface have no water above them, so they are strongly attracted downwards by the molecules below them. These attractive forces are strong enough to keep the water from spilling over the top of the glass, even when the level rises quite a bit beyond it. But eventually the volume of water above the rim of the glass becomes too great for the surface tension to hold, and the water will spill.

Minipuzzler
What happens when you add a few drops of dishwashing liquid to the water in the glass? Can you add more pennies than before, or fewer?

RED HOT TRICK

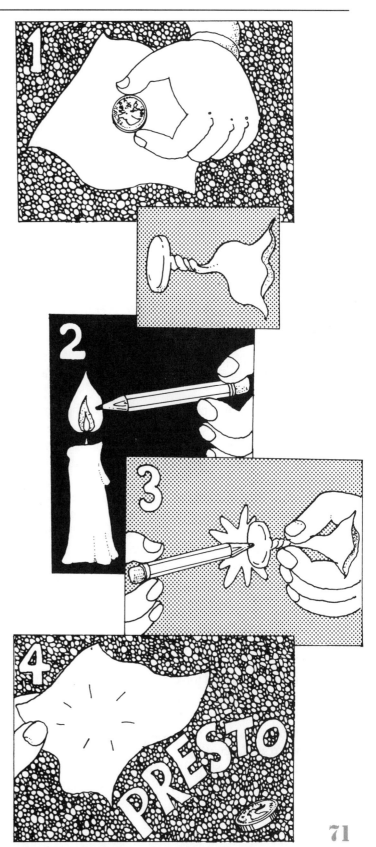

HAVE you ever tried to toast a marshmallow on the end of a wire hanger, instead of on the end of a stick? Before you've toasted many marshmallows, the wire will get too hot to hold. Here's a way to use your marshmallow-toasting experience to do an amazing feat. You can hold a piece of burning wood to a cloth without scorching it!

You'll need:
a quarter
an old cotton handkerchief or other piece of cotton
a pencil you no longer want
a candle in a candleholder

1. Place the quarter in the centre of the piece of cloth and twist the cloth so that it is stretched tightly over the coin, as shown. If the cloth is not pressed tightly enough against the coin, the material will scorch.
2. Light the candle. Hold the lead end of the pencil in the flame until the wood glows red hot.
3. Press the hot end of the pencil hard against the cloth where it covers the coin. Count to 10.
4. Remove the pencil, shake out the handkerchief, and blow away any loose ash. Presto! The cloth has not been burned.

How does it work?
Heat travels through different materials in different ways. Wood is a poor conductor of heat — heat does not travel quickly along a wooden stick. But metal is a very good conductor of heat — the heat travels quickly.

The metal in the coin is an excellent conductor of heat. It carries the heat from the smouldering wood right through the cloth so quickly that the heat has no time to scorch the material.

If the material did get scorched, you did not have the cloth pulled tightly enough against the coin. Therefore the coin was not able to conduct the heat directly from the smouldering wood.

AMAZING ROLLING CAN

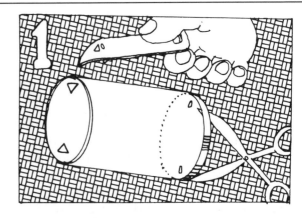

ERE'S a trick that uses rubber band power to make a can roll away from you — then back again all on its own.

You'll need:
a can "punch" opener
scissors
a coffee can or other can with a plastic lid
a long rubber band
a heavy nut or bolt

1. First, make your trick can. Use the can punch opener to make two holes on opposite sides in the end of the can. Punch matching holes in the plastic lid with a pair of scissors.
2. Cut the rubber band and feed it through the bottom holes, as shown.
3. Measure where the approximate centre of the band will be when it's stretched from end to end of the coffee can. Tie the nut or bolt to that spot so that when you're done, it will hang as shown in the illustration.
4. Thread the free ends of the band through the holes in the lid. Put the lid on the can and tie the rubber band ends together firmly on the outside of the lid.
5. Now your can is ready to perform. Roll the can away from you along level ground. When the can slows down, say, "Come to me." The can will stop — and then roll back towards you!

How does it work?
Rubber bands can store up energy and release it later. How? When you stretch or twist a rubber band, the band stores the energy it took you to stretch or twist it. When you let go, the energy is released. This trick makes use of the rubber band's ability to store and release energy. As you roll the can away from you across the ground, the weight inside the can causes the rubber band to twist, storing up energy. When the

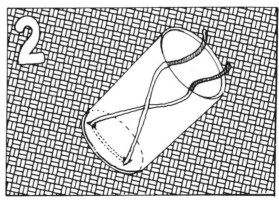

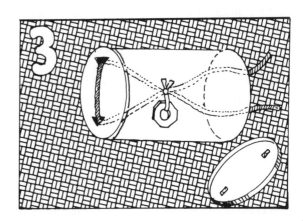

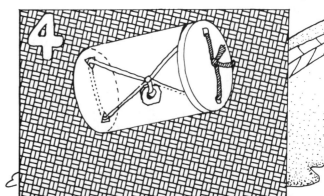

rubber band is tightly twisted, the can stops moving and starts to release its energy by rolling back towards you.

Rolling Up Hill
Make your returning can trick even more spectacular by rolling it downhill and having it apparently defy gravity by rolling back up to you. You could have it perform on a ramp by using a long board propped up at one end. Test your can first to see how far it will roll, and try to use a board long enough so the can will return before it reaches the end. Or, make a smooth junction with the floor by using cardboard so the can rolls off the ramp and comes back up it.

MAGIC WAND

JUST by combing your hair, you can make your comb appear to turn into a magic wand. Sound incredible? Try these experiments and see for yourself. It's best to try them on a dry day, and your hair should be clean.

You'll need:
a plastic or hard nylon comb
a piece of paper
a ping-pong ball

Magic Wand Trick #1

1. Turn on the cold water tap in the bathroom so that there's a thin stream of water coming from it.
2. Run your comb through your hair several times and quickly hold the comb close to the stream of water. Presto! Like magic, the stream of water bends towards the comb.

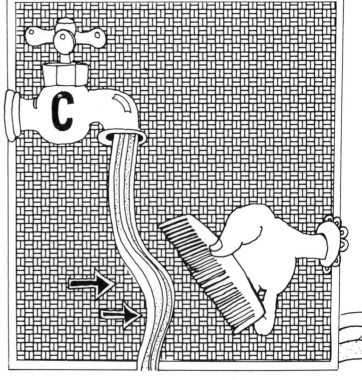

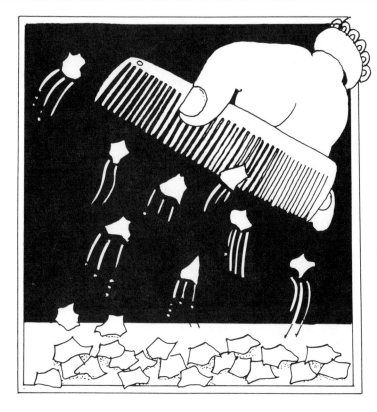

Magic Wand Trick #2

1. Tear up a piece of paper into tiny pieces.
2. Run your comb through your hair several times and quickly hold it over the paper. The bits of paper will jump up and stick to the comb.

Magic Wand Trick #3

1. "Charge" your comb by rubbing it on wool or some synthetic fabrics. (Test a variety of fabrics.) Rubbing it on a clean cat also works well.
2. Make a ping-pong ball follow you by holding your charged comb to it, and then slowly moving it forward. The ping-pong ball will roll along behind the comb.

How does it work?

All these tricks are the effects of static electricity, the same phenomenon that gives you a shock if you touch someone after shuffling across a carpet. When you run the comb through your hair (or shuffle your feet on the carpet), tiny particles called electrons move from one object to the other, leaving both with an electrical charge.

Electrically charged objects are able to attract things around them that have an opposite or neutral charge. They also repel things that have the same charge. That's why you may have noticed that, as you run the comb through your hair on a dry day, it leaves some hair standing away from your head — the hairs are charged and are repelling one another.

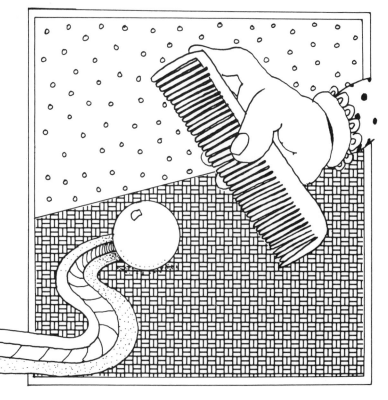

KITCHEN MAGIC

YOU can be a magician. All you need is some food! A lot of the everyday things in your kitchen can produce magical effects.

Magic potion
Try mixing up this amazing potion for your friends.

You'll need:
15 mL (1 Tbsp) baking soda
water
15 mL (1 Tbsp) vinegar
large glass

1. Mix the baking soda with the water in the glass.
2. Add the vinegar. (A few magic words will make things more dramatic.)
3. Stand back and watch.

How does it work?
One of the most common "magical" reactions in the kitchen happens when you mix an acid (such as vinegar, lemon juice or buttermilk) and a base (such as baking soda). Acids and bases shake things up wherever they go. One of the nice things they do is make gas when you mix them. The bubbles they produce make things like pancakes rise and become light and fluffy. Without them, you'd have concrete cakes!

Too much of one or the other can cause chemical reactions in certain foods—with fun results.

Rainbow brew
Here's some more magic brewing with acids and bases.

You'll need:
grape juice (*not* grape drink!)
15 mL (1 Tbsp) baking soda dissolved in 125 mL (½ c) water
15 mL (1 Tbsp) vinegar dissolved in 125 mL (½ c) water
large glass

1. Half fill the glass with grape juice.
2. Slowly pour in some of the baking soda mixture.
3. Watch what happens.
4. Slowly pour in some of the vinegar solution.
5. Try alternating them.

How does it work?
Ordinary (white) light is made up of many different colours. Depending on their molecular structure, objects absorb some, all or none of the colours of white light that hit them. The colours that aren't absorbed are reflected or passed through the object and eventually reach your eyes. The colour you see depends on which colours bounced off or passed through the object. Grape juice absorbs all the colours of white light except those that make you see purple. When you add one of your "magic" mixtures to the grape juice, you change its molecular structure, which also changes the colours that it absorbs and reflects.

Magic egg predictor
If you don't do the next magic trick right, you'll really lay an egg.

You'll need:
1 hard-boiled egg
1 uncooked egg

1. Hand a friend the two eggs and announce that you can tell the cooked egg from the raw one without even cracking the shell.
2. Put one egg at a time on a table and spin it. If it goes fast, crack it open on top of your head—it's the hard cooked one! If it spins slowly and stops quickly DON'T CRACK IT ON YOUR HEAD or the yolk will be on you.

How does it work?

The secret is in the spin. A hard-boiled egg is solid and spins as a unit. In a raw egg, you spin the shell, but the shell has to start moving the liquidy insides. This uses up energy so the egg spins slowly.

Baked ice cream

Would it take magic to bake ice cream without melting it? No. You can do it and surprise everyone with the results.

You'll need:
3 egg whites
125 mL (½ c) sugar
a big, thick, hard cookie (Chinese almond cookies work well)
250 mL (1 c) ice cream
baking sheet
aluminum foil

1. Heat oven to 260° C (500° F).
2. Cover the baking sheet with aluminum foil.
3. Beat the egg whites (do not put in the egg yolks) until they form soft peaks.

4. Add sugar to the beaten egg whites, 15 mL (1 Tbsp) at a time, beating the egg whites after each addition.
5. Continue to beat the egg whites and sugar until the mixture is thick and glossy looking. This is called meringue.
6. Put the cookie on the baking sheet. Place some frozen ice cream on top of the cookie, so that it fits without hanging over the edge of the cookie.
7. Spread meringue thickly all over the ice cream like icing on a cake, covering it completely. Make sure there are no exposed spots!
8. Ask an adult to put the baking sheet with the cookie into the oven. Bake on the lowest rack of the oven for 3 to 5 minutes until the meringue is light brown. Watch it closely so it doesn't burn.
9. Ask an adult to take the cookie out of the oven.

How does it work?

The meringue acts something like an insulated foam drinking cup, the insulation in a house or a down-filled coat. They all have small air spaces trapped in them that slow down the passage of heat or cold.

The meringue works the same way. Beating the egg whites made lots of air bubbles in the meringue. When you spread the meringue over the ice cream, you insulate it so the heat can't get in during the short time it's in the oven.

If meringue were permanent and didn't melt (or get eaten) you could probably use it to insulate a drinking cup, a house, even you. Imagine wearing a meringue parka to school. If you forgot your lunch, you could just eat your coat!

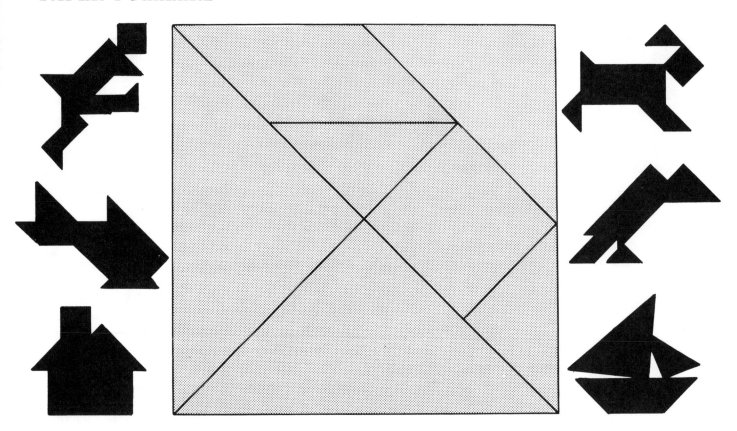

 HESE two puzzles are guaranteed to give your brain a good workout. If you get stuck, try them out on your friends and family.

You'll need:
paper
a pencil
scissors

Rubic's Cube, Move Over

This puzzle is a match for the Rubic's Cube.
1. The 12 shapes shown on the next page are all the possible arrangements of five squares. Trace them onto a piece of paper and cut them out.
2. Try to fit them into a rectangle six squares high by 10 squares long, using all 12 shapes. Stumped? You'll find one solution on page 188. But according to a computer, there are 2338 other ways. If you figure out all 2338 other ways, you may be eligible for *The Guinness Book of Records*.

Tangram Puzzle

Here's how to make a challenging geometrical puzzle called a tangram.

1. Trace the square above onto a piece of paper.
2. Cut out along the black lines to make seven pieces, or "tans."
3. Choose one of the drawings and try to make it using all seven tans. Stumped? Keep trying different combinations before you check your solution on page 188. Once you've mastered all of the tangram puzzlers given, see how many figures you can create with the tans.

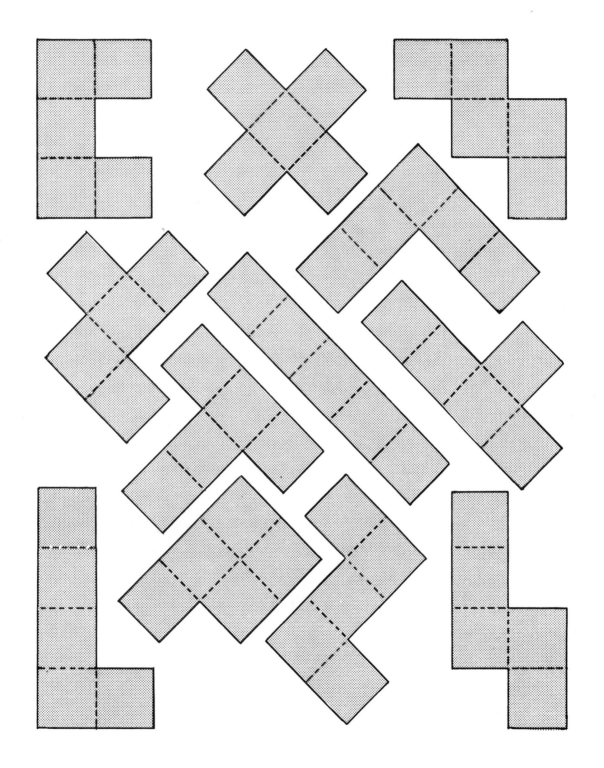

SCIENCE THAT GROWS ON YOU

THE SECRET LIFE OF SEEDS

WHAT do peas, rice, peanuts, corn, beans, wheat and nuts have in common? Besides the fact that you eat them, they're all seeds.

Seeds are more than just a way to grow food: many seeds actually are food themselves! For example, some seeds are used to season food, such as anise, caraway, coriander, dill, pepper and celery seeds. Others, like corn and peanuts, are squeezed to make oil. Still others make great snacks when roasted—for example, pumpkin and sunflower seeds.

Although they don't have legs to help them get around, aren't clever like some animals and can't fight off predators, seeds have talents few people notice.

Most seeds (except an impatient few) are able to wait for exactly the right moment before germinating, or beginning to grow. This can mean a wait of one year, ten years, even 85 years. Seeds found after several thousand years in the tombs of Egyptian pharaohs or kings were still able to germinate!

This talent means that a seed can wait for everything to be just right—water, temperature, light, oxygen—before taking the big plunge and sending out a shoot.

A lot of things can set a seed off sprouting. Most seeds germinate after a dormant, or inactive, period.

Some seeds' growth is triggered by light. Some will grow only after a certain amount of rain. This is helpful in desert areas. Since plants need water to survive, sprouting after a lot of rain at least gives them a good start.

Other seeds, such as those from some water plants, are dormant until freezing and thawing cracks their outer coating or water wears it away. Still others, such as jack pine, germinate only after being exposed to extreme heat. These seeds are the first to sprout after a forest fire, bringing the forest back to life.

A lot of seeds grow only after being exposed to a cold spell. This keeps the plant from sprouting in the summer or fall when it wouldn't have a long enough season to grow.

Without legs, seeds have to be ingenious to get around. Animals and birds often unknowingly help seeds spread. For example, when squirrels store nuts for future meals, they sometimes forget where they bury them, leaving a trail of trees and plants to mark their absent-mindedness. When birds eat berries, they can't digest the seeds and excrete them after flying far away from the original plant.

Some seeds are "hitchhikers." They have small hooks or barbs to attach themselves to any animal—

including you—that comes by. They get carried off to other locations and dropped there.

"Parachuters," such as dandelions, and "winged" seeds, such as those from maple trees, are so light that they are blown easily from place to place.

"Shooting" seeds are formed in pods which burst open and fire them out.

Seed bank

You won't find any tellers in a seed bank. Instead you'll find seeds from thousands of different plants stored on temperature-controlled shelves.

Why are seeds "banked?" Many countries store seeds in seed banks in case an agricultural disease or some other disaster wipes out or threatens certain plants. Seeds are also saved in case anyone ever wants to use an old strain that's no longer being grown.

Of course, seeds can't be stored forever. When they start to get old they are planted so new seeds can be produced and saved.

Seed stroll

Here's a simple way to collect seeds. Put an old pair of wool socks over your shoes and walk through a vacant lot or woods. Hitchhiking seeds will hang on to you just like they do on an animal's coat. You can pick them off with tweezers later to study them.

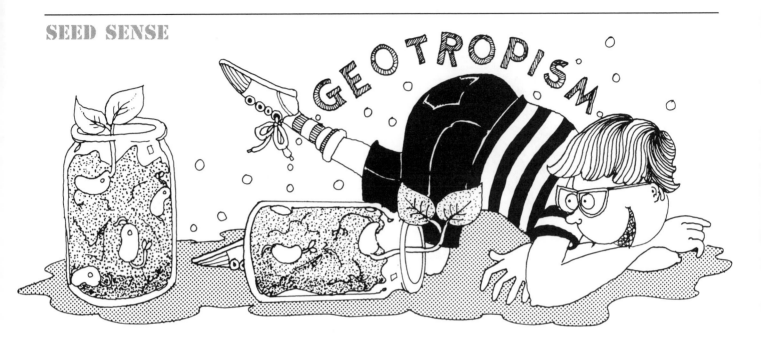

GEOTROPISM

OES it matter which way you plant a seed? After all, you want the plant's stem to grow up and the roots to grow down. Will the plant know which way to grow if you place the seed upside down? You can find out by making some glass gardens.

You'll need:
10 fresh beans (any kind, either from the supermarket or from a seed packet)
two wide-mouthed jars or glasses
a piece of blotting paper big enough to line the inside of both jars
paper towels

1. Soak the beans in water overnight.
2. Cut the blotting paper to fit snugly around the inside of each jar.
3. Stuff the middle of the jars with crumpled paper towels, then fill them with water and let the paper soak it up until it is saturated and will absorb no more. Pour off the remaining water.
4. Push five of the soaked seeds between the blotting paper and the glass in each jar, spacing them out evenly and keeping them near the top of the jars. Place the seeds in different positions — horizontal, vertical, and diagonal.

5. Put the jars where you can watch them for several days, but keep them out of direct sunlight. The blotting paper must be kept moist for the seeds to grow, so water the paper towels regularly. Over the next few days, you can watch the seeds germinate. Roots will grow from one end of each seed, and a stem from the other end, but no matter which way you placed the seeds, the roots will turn down and the stems will turn up. In less than a week, the seeds will have little green leaves.
6. After the seedlings have grown an inch above the top of the jars, lay one of the jars on its side. In a few days you'll see the stems are growing upward again, and the roots have bent to keep growing down!

How does it work?
There are growth hormones in plants that respond to the Earth's gravitational pull and make roots grow down and stems grow up. This response is called geotropism (Greek for "turning to earth"), and that's why you don't have to worry about planting seeds right side up.

WATER FLOWING UP-TREE MYSTERY

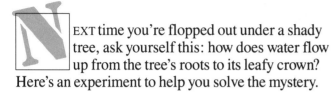EXT time you're flopped out under a shady tree, ask yourself this: how does water flow up from the tree's roots to its leafy crown? Here's an experiment to help you solve the mystery.

You'll need:
a cup, half-filled with water
some blue or red food colouring
a stalk of celery with some leaves on it

1. Mix a teaspoon of the food colouring into the water.
2. Cut the celery stalk about 2 cm (about 1 inch) from the bottom to expose a fresh end and stand the stalk in the water.
3. Leave the celery in the water for an hour or two and you'll see the dye gradually colouring the leaves.
4. When the colour has spread to the tips of the leaves, take the celery out of the water and cut across the stalk. You'll see a row of tiny circles outlined in colour — they're the cut ends of fine long tubes that travel the length of the stalk. The coloured water travelled up those tubes. Trees have similar tubes running up their trunks.

How does it work?
What makes the water climb the trees is still somewhat of a mystery. But scientists think it all depends on the special properties of water, and on the fact that the tubes are porous and very narrow. As the tubes spread out into the leaves, heat from the sun evaporates the water molecules at the top. Because water tends to climb a short way up the walls of certain substances (like drinking glasses, for instance), the next molecules in line move up after those that evaporate. Water molecules always hold tightly together, and when they're squished into very narrow tubes, they grip even more tightly, with enough strength to pull all the following water molecules along behind them. So as the molecules at the top move up, the whole chain moves up the tree. This only works, however, if the tubes are full of liquid to begin with, so trees and other plants have liquid-filled tubes from their earliest days as seedlings.

MAKING SOIL

OU may think the stuff that you wash off your hands is the very same stuff that plants can't live without—dirt. But you're only partly right.

Actually, dirt is almost useless to a plant. It's only finely ground rocks and minerals. What plants need is *soil*. Soil is dirt with character.

To get soil you mix dirt with decayed plants and animals (decomposed organic matter), air and water. The organic matter gives plants about 10 per cent of their nourishment. The rest comes from the atmosphere.

Who cares about the difference between dirt and soil? Plants do! Most plants can't thrive in dirt with a lot of coarse sand, gravel or stone. It just won't hold the nutrients and water they need to survive. Soil that contains a lot of clay, however, *will* hold these things, and plants thrive like Jack's magic beanstalk.

What else does soil contain that plants need? If you could scoop up half a hectare (an acre) of typical farm soil down to a depth of 15 cm (6 inches), you'd find:

- 1-2 tonnes (tons) of fungi—organisms that live on dead matter
- 1-2 tonnes (tons) of bacteria—creatures that have only a single cell
- 90 kg (200 pounds) of one-celled animals called protozoa
- 45 kg (100 pounds) of tiny water plants called algae
- 45 kg (100 pounds) of yeasts, which are microscopic plant/animals.

These help break down the organic matter in soil so the plants can pull the nutrients out of it.

How thick is the soil on Earth? Think of the world as a tomato. The skin of the tomato compared to its size is much, much thicker than the layer of soil covering the Earth compared to its size.

That sounds like a pretty thin layer of soil—and it is. Because it is so thin, loss of topsoil, or "erosion," is a major problem in the world. It's estimated that 75 billion tonnes (tons) of soil are lost in the world every year—just about 1 per cent of all the topsoil there is.

When good soil rich in nutrients is blown away by wind or washed away by heavy rains, it eventually ends up in the ocean where it stays forever. It can take from 100 to 2500 years for the natural wearing down of rocks and collection of nutrients to make 2.5 cm (1 inch) of topsoil. It only takes 10 years to lose it. If too much soil is lost, all that's left is a desert.

Erosion can be controlled by taking care of the soil. Plants help anchor soil in place. Their roots help hold the topsoil down so that it can't blow or wash away. With some care in planting and by keeping forests from being cut down or marshes from being drained, the harmful effects of erosion can be reduced.

A dirty job

In nature, it takes hundreds of years to make soil. You can make your own in just a matter of minutes. The trick? You can use a hammer: nature can't.

You'll need:
cheesecloth or an old cotton tea towel
very small stones (limestone or sandstone work best) or a brick (not asphalt—it contains petroleum products and will not work for this experiment)
a hammer
peat moss (buy at a hardware store or garden centre)
plant leftovers (cut-up fruit or vegetable skins, tea leaves, coffee grounds)
broken or crushed eggshells
water

1. Completely wrap the rocks in the cheesecloth or tea towel.
2. Pound and pound and pound the rocks with the hammer until they're smashed into tiny bits about the size of a grain of sugar. It will take you about 5 to 10 minutes of pounding.
3. Once the rocks are pulverized, add an equal amount of peat moss to them. (Or use half sand and half peat moss.) Peat moss conditions the soil and helps it to hold water.
4. Add the plant leftovers and broken eggshells.
5. Add some water and mix it all together.
   Is this really soil? To find out, see if a plant will grow in it. Put the mixture in a jar and plant a bean seed in it. Leave it in the sun and keep it moist. Does it grow?

A DIRTLESS GARDEN

How do you grow a garden without lots of good dirty dirt? With hydroponics. Its name tells you its secret. It comes from *hydro*, the Greek word for water, and *ponos*, the Greek word for labour—letting water do the work of soil. With your help, of course.

Make your own hydroponic garden
You'll need:
a jar with a wide mouth
a plastic flower pot, styrofoam cup or other container that can rest just inside the mouth of the jar without falling in
a piece of cotton rope long enough to reach the bottom of the jar and up into the pot as shown
seeds—radish, lettuce, spinach, peas or green beans work best
vermiculite (granite that has been expanded under pressure. Available at garden centres)
plant nutrient (called hydroponic fertilizer. Available at garden centres)

1. Fray both ends of the rope. This is your "wick."
2. Put the rope through the bottom of your flower pot or other container so that it comes about 2/3 of the way up the container and the rest hangs down below. Hold it there while you fill the pot with vermiculite.
3. Make the plant nutrient by mixing the hydroponic fertilizer with water. Read the package directions to find out how much water to add.
4. Put enough nutrient into the jar so that when you sit the flower pot in the jar mouth, the liquid isn't touching the pot.
5. Sit the pot on the jar, letting the wick hang into the nutrient solution.
6. Plant your seeds in the vermiculite. Not too deep! Depending on the plant you have chosen and the size of your pot, you can plant two or three seeds in the pot. Just make sure the planting spots are 7-8 cm (about 3 inches) apart. It's a good idea to put two seeds at each spot, to make sure you get a sprout.
7. Put your vegetable garden in a window that gets a lot of sun every day. Make sure there's always enough nutrient solution in the jar to keep the wick wet. Plain water won't work: your plants will starve without the nutrients in the fertilizer.

Now watch it grow! Even though you haven't used soil, your seeds should sprout up in two to three weeks. If they're too crowded, pull out a few of the plants so they have 5-7 cm (about 2 inches) between them. Soon you'll be eating food from your own garden.

How does it work?
Soil provides *support* for the plants and *food* for them to grow. You've used vermiculite to support the plants and substituted fertilizer for the food they'd normally get from the decayed plants and animals in soil.

The wick, with its frayed ends, creates a kind of highway for the food and water to travel up to the plant's root area. With all these things, plus lots of sun, you've created an ideal environment for your plants.

Hydroponics then and now

Hydroponics isn't a new idea. It was used in the Hanging Gardens of Babylon thousands of years ago. The ancient Aztecs and the Chinese also used hydroponics.

Today many hydroponic greenhouses grow vegetables year-round in areas where seasonal changes make it impossible to grow them in the ground. Restaurants frequently serve hydroponically grown vegetables, particularly lettuce. Not only is it available locally and fresh all the time, but it's clean too. (Vermiculite doesn't stick to plants the way soil does.) And since the plants are being grown in a controlled environment, they're also free of insects and insecticides.

The only thing that's wrong with hydroponic gardening is that it doesn't give you a good excuse to get your hands dirty!

89

IF you left a pair of socks out in the yard this summer and forgot about them, what would you expect to find next spring when you went looking for them? That would depend on what they were made of — and on whether your dog found them first! To get an idea of what you might find, you can plant a reverse garden — reverse, because most people plant gardens to see things grow; you're planting this one to see things fall apart.

You'll need:
an old nylon stocking
some cotton cloth (an old sock or piece of towel will do, but make sure it's 100% cotton)
a piece of paper
some plastic wrap
some wool
a styrofoam or plastic cup
a piece of aluminum foil
an apple core

1. Dig a 12 cm (5 inches) deep hole for each item you're planting.
2. Pour enough water into each hole to thoroughly dampen the earth, then place one article in each hole and cover it with dirt. Be sure to put a marker over each item so you can find it again.
3. Leave the articles in your garden for 30 days and water them every day. At the end of that time, dig them up. How have things changed?

What happened?
Some of the things you "planted" have started to disintegrate. They are biodegradable — natural organisms can break them apart. What about the things that haven't disintegrated? Do you notice any similarities among them?

Be a Super Camper
Next time you're out camping, think of your reverse garden before you throw anything out. The two lists below show you which things are biodegradable and which aren't. Before you leave your campsite, you should bury the biodegradable things in a pit to speed up disintegration. Take the non-biodegradable garbage home with you.

Bury	*Take home*
food	plastic wrap
paper (you can	styrofoam cups
burn this)	or trays
	aluminum foil
	plastic bottles
	cans

THE WHEAT GAME

BEING a farmer has to be one of the world's greatest jobs! You're outside in the sunshine all day, riding around on your tractor, wearing your most comfortable clothes. You grow your own food, so you don't have to worry about going to the store. As far as growing food is concerned, what could be easier? All you have to do is plant a seed and watch it grow. Right? Not quite.

To give you a better sense of what farming is really like, try playing The Wheat Game on the next page.

Wheat is the world's largest crop. One-seventh of all farm land around the world is used for growing wheat. Every moment of the year some farmer, somewhere, is harvesting wheat, and another one is planting it.

Here's your chance to see what farming is really like, and you don't even have to get dirty—or develop any blisters.

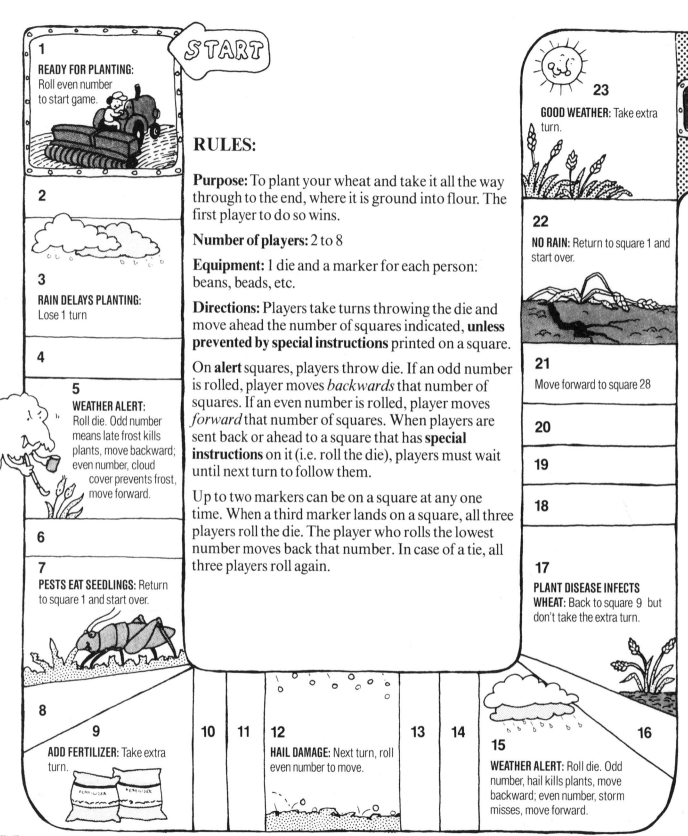

1 READY FOR PLANTING: Roll even number to start game.

2

3 RAIN DELAYS PLANTING: Lose 1 turn

4

5 WEATHER ALERT: Roll die. Odd number means late frost kills plants, move backward; even number, cloud cover prevents frost, move forward.

6

7 PESTS EAT SEEDLINGS: Return to square 1 and start over.

8

9 ADD FERTILIZER: Take extra turn.

10

11

12 HAIL DAMAGE: Next turn, roll even number to move.

13

14

15 WEATHER ALERT: Roll die. Odd number, hail kills plants, move backward; even number, storm misses, move forward.

16

17 PLANT DISEASE INFECTS WHEAT: Back to square 9 but don't take the extra turn.

18

19

20

21 Move forward to square 28

22 NO RAIN: Return to square 1 and start over.

23 GOOD WEATHER: Take extra turn.

RULES:

Purpose: To plant your wheat and take it all the way through to the end, where it is ground into flour. The first player to do so wins.

Number of players: 2 to 8

Equipment: 1 die and a marker for each person: beans, beads, etc.

Directions: Players take turns throwing the die and move ahead the number of squares indicated, **unless prevented by special instructions** printed on a square.

On **alert** squares, players throw die. If an odd number is rolled, player moves *backwards* that number of squares. If an even number is rolled, player moves *forward* that number of squares. When players are sent back or ahead to a square that has **special instructions** on it (i.e. roll the die), players must wait until next turn to follow them.

Up to two markers can be on a square at any one time. When a third marker lands on a square, all three players roll the die. The player who rolls the lowest number moves back that number. In case of a tie, all three players roll again.

24 RAIN DELAY: Too much rain slows growth. Next turn, roll even number to move.

25

26 PEST ALERT: Roll die. Odd number, many locusts eat crop, move backward; even number, few locusts, little damage, move forward.

WARNING

27

28 WEATHER ALERT: Roll die. Odd number, heat damages plants, move backward; even number, good rainfall, move forward.

29

30 PLANT DISEASE: Wheat turns black. Back to square 9 , but don't take the extra turn.

31 ORGANIZE HARVEST: Lose 1 turn.

Fix combine ✓
oil auger ✓
repair bins ✓
order parts
for tractor

32 EQUIPMENT ALERT: Roll die. Odd number, tractor broken, move backward; even number, tractor repaired, move forward.

33

34 RAIN DELAY: Fields too muddy to harvest. Next turn must roll even number to move.

35 EXTRA FARM HANDS HIRED: Ahead 4.

36

37 FARM HAND QUITS: Back 1.

38 FIRE DESTROYS CROP: Start over.

39

40 PREPARE TO MEET BUYER: Lose 1 turn.

41 SELLING ALERT: Roll die. Odd number, price too low, move backward; even number, good price, move forward.

42

43 EQUIPMENT ALERT: Roll die. Odd number, you can't afford new truck to ship grain, move backward; even number, you can buy truck, move forward.

44

45

RATS INFEST STORAGE SHED: Lose 1 turn.

46 RAIL STRIKE: Lose 1 turn.

ON STRIKE

47 BUYER CANCELS ORDER: Back to 40

48 SHIPPING DELAY: Must roll even number to move.

49

50 WHEAT GROUND INTO FLOUR: Game over.

FINISH

FLOUR

PLANTING AN IDEA

How many plants have you eaten in the past week? 10? 30? 100? 200? (Don't forget to count the "hidden" plants like the grains in bread and crackers.)

If you're like everyone else, you probably ate about 30.

From 300 000 to 100

There are about 300 000 plants in the world, but only about 30 000 are known to be edible by people. And only a hundred or so are actually grown and eaten on a regular basis somewhere in the world.

Why do people eat so few? We eat the hundred plants that were first domesticated early in history. Other plants were harder to grow, so people didn't bother with them. Instead they stuck with the first easy-to-grow hundred. Why experiment when you have something that works?

30 favourites

Out of the hundred plants that are commonly eaten, people in any part of the world usually eat only about 30. Why?

The main reason is that people mostly eat the plants that grow easily where they live. Of course, with modern transportation and storage, people have more variety available today. Food can be brought from all over the world to your local grocery store so you no longer have to eat just what is grown nearby. But still, local customs frequently determine what people eat.

The Big Four

The four plants people eat most of are wheat, rice, corn and potatoes. They provide more than half of the world's food from plants. More than one-third of the people in the world use wheat as a staple (main) food and one-third use rice.

How did these four plants become so popular? Years ago, people experimented with different plants. They discovered that wheat, rice, corn and potatoes

were the most nutritious. They were also easy to grow, travelled well and produced the greatest amount of food.

People don't always choose the most nutritious plants as the main part of their diets. In Africa, many people grow and eat a root vegetable called cassava. It's not especially nutritious. In fact, many people are malnourished because cassava is the main part of their diet. It's still used a lot, though, because it's easy to grow, even in poor soil.

Count the plants
Keep a list of all the different plants you eat in a week. See if you can eat twice as many different plants next week. Ask a friend whose family is from a different culture to do the same and compare your lists.

THE GREAT OUTDOORS

COOL IT!

ow can you keep cool on those hot summer days? It's a snap with some simple science.

You'll need:
a pair of socks
some water
a warm, dry day

1. Soak one sock in water and then wring out the excess water.
2. Take the socks and your feet outside, put on the socks (one wet, one dry), and sit with your feet in the sun. Do you notice any temperature difference between your feet?

How does it work?
Your wet foot feels cooler thanks to evaporation. Evaporation is the process that uses energy to turn a liquid into a gas. Whenever liquid evaporates from a surface, heat is used up so the surface becomes cooler. And that's what happens to your foot. The evaporating water uses heat from the sun and your body. The result: cooler tootsies.

Evaporation is also what makes you feel cooler when a fan blows at you. The moving air makes perspiration evaporate more quickly. In fact, the cooling effect of evaporation is one of the reasons we perspire.

WHAT does science have to do with fashion? Look around. As winter approaches and the weather gets cooler, people change into warmer, heavier clothes. These clothes have something else in common besides weight and warmth: they're usually much darker in colour than summer clothes. Navy blue, brown, dark greens, and dark reds are the colours of winter clothes, instead of pastels and white of summer. That makes good science sense, as this experiment shows.

You'll need:
2 white paper cups
a weather or cooking thermometer
some black paint

1. Paint the outside of one cup black.
2. Pour equal amounts of water (at the same temperature) into both cups and stand them side by side in the sun for about half an hour.
3. Test the temperature of the water in both cups. Which is warmer?

How does it work?
Don't be surprised if the water in the black cup is warmer. Dark colours absorb light and change it to heat. Light colours, on the other hand, act like reflectors and bounce light off. That's why it makes good science sense to wear dark, heat-absorbing colours in winter and light heat-reflecting colours in summer.

S OLAR-POWERED clocks were invented thousands of years ago and you can make one. It's called a sundial.

The metric measurements cannot be converted into exact Imperial equivalents. For this project only, use the measurements for centimetres interchangeably with inches. A sundial built in inches will be more than twice as big as one built in centimetres.

You'll need:

2 pieces of heavy corrugated cardboard 20 cm (inches) square (Wood is better if you're going to leave it outside, but you'll need help sawing.)
a compass
a pen
a ruler
a protractor
scissors
white glue
masking tape

1. On one piece of cardboard 20 cm (inches) square, draw two diagonal lines from corner to corner, as shown. Where they meet is the centre of the cardboard.
2. Adjust the compass so that the point and the pencil are 9 cm (inches) apart, and draw a circle by putting the compass point in the centre of the cardboard. You should now have a circle 18 cm (inches) across.
3. Divide the circle in half and mark off 12 equally-spaced points around the circumference of one half. Number each point in this order, as shown: 6, 7, 8, 9, 10, 11, 12, 1, 2, 3, 4, 5. This is your dial.
4. Now you can start work on the triangular marker, called a gnomon (that's Greek for "one who knows"). On the second piece of cardboard, draw a line 8 cm (inches) long for the gnomon's base.
5. To make your sundial work properly, it must have the same angle as the latitude where you live. Use the Latitude Finder on the next page to get the correct angle for your gnomon. When you have it, use a protractor to mark off the angle at one end of the baseline, as shown.
6. Draw a line 20 cm (inches) long, from the end of the base through the mark, and connect the end of that line to the other end of the base. Cut out the gnomon.
7. On the dial, draw a line from the number 12 to the centre of the circle and mark a point 1 cm (inch) from the centre. Place the base of the gnomon along this line, with the measured angle touching the mark. Glue and tape it in place, and your sundial is ready.
8. Pick a spot for it where the sun shines all day, but — oddly enough — you'll have to wait until night to set it up. That's because the tip of the gnomon must point to the north, and the best way to do that is to line it up with the North Star (that's the bright one at the end of the Little Dipper's handle). Sight along the slant of the gnomon until the tip points to the star, then fix your sundial in place so it can't easily be moved.
9. To tell the time with your sundial, look at the shadow cast by the gnomon. The number on the dial where the edge of the shadow falls, is the correct time.

Why does the gnomon have to be at an angle?
Because the Earth is tilted on its axis, the sun appears to be lower on the horizon in the winter and higher in the summer. This apparent shift forms an angle with the horizon at sunset and sunrise. Wherever you are, that angle is equal to your latitude. If you build the gnomon of your sundial so that it forms the same angle with the base, the shadow will always fall in the same spot at the same time, all year round.

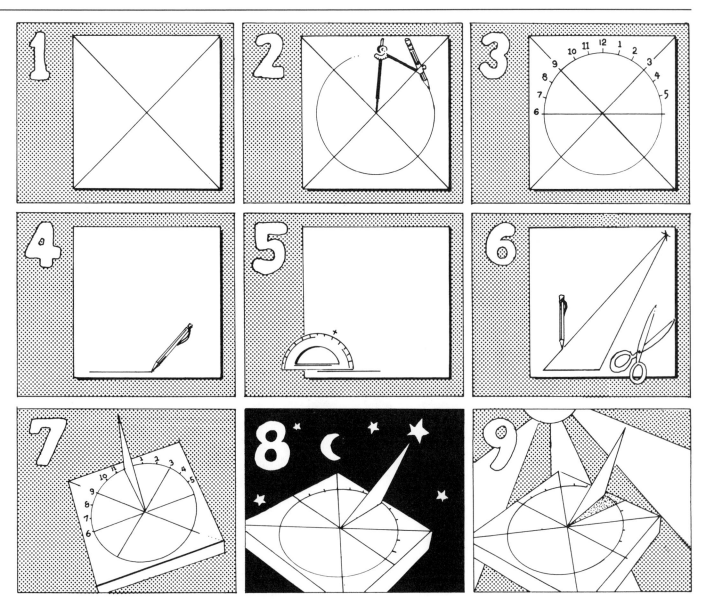

LATITUDE FINDER

City	Latitude*	City	Latitude*	City	Latitude*
Vancouver, B.C.	49 N	Montreal, Quebec	43 N	Chicago, Illinois	41 N
Edmonton, Alberta	53 N	Quebec City, Quebec	46 N	Houston, Texas	29 N
Calgary, Alberta	51 N	Halifax, Nova Scotia	44 N	New Orleans, Louisiana	30 N
Winnipeg, Manitoba	50 N	St. John's, Newfoundland	47 N	Washington, D.C.	39 N
Toronto, Ontario	44 N			New York City, New York	40 N
Ottawa, Ontario	45 N	Los Angeles, California	34 N		
		Minneapolis, Minnesota	45 N		

NOTE: If you can't find your home town here, look in an atlas.   *rounded off to nearest degree.

How can you get rid of the dirt in muddy water? Put it in the laundry? Strain it? The easiest way is to make this simple water purifier and let the sun do it.

You'll need:
a large pan or tub
a glass shorter than the pan
2 small, clean rocks
a piece of clear plastic food wrap big enough to fit over the pan
masking tape

1. Fill the pan to a depth of 5 cm (2 inches) with muddy water.
2. Set it where the sun will shine on it all day.
3. Put the glass right-side up in the centre of the pan and anchor it down, if necessary, by putting a small, clean rock in it.
4. Cover the pan with clear plastic. Pull it tight and tape it firmly to the pan.

5. Put a rock on the plastic wrap over the centre of the glass (don't let the rock touch the glass), then watch what happens. During the day, drops of clean water will form inside the plastic film and drip into the glass.

How does it work?

The sun's warmth heats the water, making it evaporate (turn into water vapour). When the vapour touches the cooler plastic wrap, it condenses back into water droplets. You have purified the water through a process called distillation. But what happened to the mud?

The dirt and stuff that make up mud don't evaporate at the same temperature that water does. So when the water vaporizes, it leaves the particles of mud behind. The water you collect in the cup has very few impurities.

Distillation is often used when the substances in a mixture have to be separated. For instance, it's one way of making fresh water out of salt water.

EARTH SPEEDOMETER

E all know that the Earth turns — that's what makes the sun appear to move across the sky. Here's a way to clock the Earth's speed using an easy-to-make solar speedometer.

You'll need:
a magnifying glass
masking tape
a chair
a piece of white paper
a watch or clock with a second hand

1. Tape the handle of the magnifying glass to the seat of the chair so the lens extends horizontally over the edge, and place it in the sun.
2. Put the paper where the light passing through the lens shines on the ground. Raise the paper closer to the lens, or lift the chair to move the lens farther away from the paper, until you get a sharp circle of light, then use books or boxes to prop up the paper or the chair.
3. Draw a tight circle around the spot of light, then use your watch or clock to time how long it takes for the light to entirely leave the circle.

What's happening?
The spot of light is actually a tiny picture of the sun. When it moves fully out of the circle you have drawn around it, the Earth has travelled ½° of its 360° rotation. If you multiply the time it took for your "sunspot" to move that ½° by 720 and figure it out in hours, you'll find out approximately how long the day really is. Astronomers use atomic clocks to measure the exact length of the day.

Sun Catching
Solar energy is often collected with lenses or reflectors. You've seen how quickly the spot of sunlight moves, so you can imagine how difficult it is to keep the light falling directly onto the solar collectors. The most common solution to this problem is the use of motors to turn the solar collectors at the same speed as the Earth rotates, only in the opposite direction. This way, they point directly at the sun all day.

WHERE DOES THE WIND COME FROM?

ID you ever wonder what makes the wind? Here's an experiment that turns an ordinary light bulb into a wind-making machine.

You'll need:
a lamp
talcum powder

1. Remove the lamp's shade and turn on the lamp.
2. When the bulb is hot, sprinkle a tiny bit of talcum powder just above it, and watch what happens.

How does it work?
The powder is carried upwards by a rising current of warm air, or wind, warmed by the light bulb. Real wind starts when the sun heats the earth. As the earth gets warm, it heats the air just above it. This hot air expands, making it lighter. The warm, light air rises, leaving room for heavier, cooler air to move in and take its place. This movement of air is what we call wind.

YOU'LL need:
a light bulb
a pencil
a piece of paper
scissors

1. Cut a spiral out of the piece of paper, as shown.
2. Balance the centre of the spiral on the point of a pencil. You may have to make a small indentation in the paper to keep it from slipping off, but be careful not to make a hole.
3. Turn on the light bulb and wait a few minutes until it is hot. Then hold your pencil with the balanced spiral just above the bulb. What happens?

How does it work?
The spiral started to spin because the hot light bulb warmed the air around it. This hot light air started rising, creating a mini-wind that spins the spiral like the real wind spins a pinwheel.

cut paper spiral

2.

"IT's raining, it's pouring . . ." goes the old song. But where does all that rain come from? One way to find out is by making some rain in your own kitchen.

You'll need:
a large metal spoon or soup ladle
a kettle one-quarter filled with water

1. Put the spoon or ladle into the freezer to cool it.
2. When the spoon is ice cold, turn on the kettle. (Don't take the spoon out of the freezer until the water boils.) As the water in the kettle heats up, it turns into steam. Most people think the white vapour coming from the kettle is steam, but it's not. Real steam is invisible. If you look carefully — but not too closely — at the spout, you'll see a space between the kettle spout and where the white vapour starts. In that space is steam. As steam meets the air outside the kettle, it cools and becomes water vapour which is visible as a white cloud.
3. When the water is boiling, hold the cold spoon in the white vapour coming from the kettle's spout. Presto! In a few seconds it'll be "raining" in your kitchen.

How does it work?
Your cold spoon suddenly cools the water vapour that's coming from the kettle spout, making it condense into water and fall to the floor as "rain."

The Real Thing

Real rain is made in much the same way as homemade rain, but more gradually. Instead of a stove, there is the sun, which warms water in Earth's rivers, lakes, oceans, and even puddles. Fortunately for fish, frogs, and swimmers, not enough of the sun's heat reaches the Earth to make the water boil, but it is warm enough to allow tiny molecules of water to escape and rise into the sky. This is called "evaporation."

As the water-bearing warm air rises, it cools, and a cloud of water vapour forms, just like the cloud of water vapour formed when you boiled the kettle of water.

Cold air can't hold as much water as warm air. So when the air gets too cool to hold all the water vapour in it, some of the water falls back to earth as rain or snow. Then the cycle begins all over again.

HIT A HOMER: FIND THE SWEET SPOT

F someone told you that a baseball bat had a sweet spot, would you say, "Make mine chocolate"?

Well, don't get too hungry because what makes this spot sweet is the love ballplayers have for it—it's the point on the bat that makes the ball travel farthest.

How do you find it? Not by tasting the wood, but by applying this test.

You'll need:
a baseball bat
a baseball

1. Hold a wooden bat near the handle as shown between the thumb and index finger of one hand. If you have an aluminum bat, hold it about one-quarter of the distance from the top.
2. Take the baseball in your other hand and tap it against the bat's handle just below where you're holding it. You'll feel the wood vibrating in your hand. (An aluminum bat not only vibrates, it hums!)
3. Continue tapping as you move down the barrel to the fat end. Somewhere along the bat you'll find a spot where your tapping won't cause the bat to vibrate or move in your hand. You've found the sweet spot!

Many things vibrate when hit. However, every vibrating object has one or two places where the vibrations are very small and are hardly noticeable. These quiet areas are called nodes. The sweet spot is near a node.

Once you've found the sweet spot on your bat, mark it and then have a friend pitch you a few balls. You'll find that hitting a ball with the sweet spot feels better. Your hit will seem effortless, and your hand won't sting the way it does when you hit

a ball with other parts of the bat. It will even have a satisfying sound—a clear and solid "crack."

Why does the sweet spot feel so sweet?

You'll need:
a baseball
a bat
a friend

1. Crouch down and hold the baseball bat out in front of you.
2. Have your friend drop the baseball so that it hits the bat at various points. Watch how high the ball bounces each time. At what point on the bat does the ball bounce highest?

A moving bat and a moving ball each carry with them a lot of energy. When the two collide, the question always is: will their energy combine to launch the ball as far as possible into the park, or will some of it be wasted? Hitting a ball with the bat's sweet spot puts most of the energy into giving the ball a good, sound launch. Hitting anywhere else on the bat wastes some energy by transferring the energy into vibrations and movement of the bat.

Baseball bats aren't the only pieces of sports equipment with sweet spots. Tennis rackets, ping-pong paddles and even golf clubs have them. Can you find them?

Sweet spots are sometimes called joy spots. You may have heard that sports equipment manufacturers make it easy to find the sweet spot by sticking the label on top of it. Sometimes this is true, sometimes not. The only reliable way to find the sweet spot is to use the above test.

The Care and Feeding of Bats

- Don't pound home plate or the ground with your bat.
- Don't leave your bat out in the rain. Moisture warps the wood and raises the grain.
- If the grain on your bat is raised, rub it down with a smooth bone or a piece of hard wood. This is called burnishing.
- Rub oil into the bat whenever it gets wet, and also before putting it away for the winter.
- Store your bat in a cool, dry place and keep it in a vertical position. If possible, hang the bat from the beams in a dry cellar.

You'll need:
an ice-cube
a medium or large paper-clip

1. Open the paper-clip so you have a relatively straight piece of wire.
2. Put the ice-cube on a dish or paper towel.
3. Place the straightened paper-clip across the ice-cube. Hold on to the ends and press down hard for several minutes.

AH, there's nothing like a cold winter day when you can zoom downhill on your water skis. WATER SKIS?????

Yup. When you get down to it, every skier is a water skier. Downhill and cross-country skiers may think they're gliding on snow, but really they're slipping over a thin film of water. When skis rub against the snow they create friction, which melts the snow into water. Without this layer of moisture, snow skis couldn't slide—they'd be snowbound.

You've probably seen curlers furiously sweeping the ice with a broom. It's not because the ice is dusty. Sweeping the bristles against the ice also produces a thin film of water on which the curling rock slides. Toboggans, bobsleds and sleighs—they, too, glide over water.

Ice skates also travel across a film of water. The friction caused as you glide melts the ice slightly. But there's a little more to ice skating than just friction. Ice skating is a bit of a high pressure sport. Skate blades are so thin that your weight is concentrated on a very small area of the ice. This pressure alone can melt ice as you can see for yourself.

The pressure you're putting on the ice-cube creates a layer of water, just as it does under your skates. Because the melted ice-water is still very cold, it will start to refreeze around the paper-clip. (If it doesn't, it's probably because the room you're in is too warm. Try the same experiment outside on a cold day.)

The Amazing Wire Through Ice Illusion

You'll need:

a large coffee can

1 m (1 yard) picture wire

2 bricks or other similar weights

winter: this experiment works best when the temperature is between 0°C (32°F) and −10°C (14°F).

1. Fill the can almost to the top with water and freeze it.
2. Tie a brick to each end of the picture wire.
3. Run the ice-filled coffee can under warm water until the block of ice will slide out of the can. Take the ice block outside and stand it on a railing or a piece of wood or a couple of bricks so that when the picture wire is laid across the top of the ice block, the bricks tied to either end hang straight down.

4. Leave it there until the wire works its way about half-way down the ice block. (This could take a day or more depending on the temperature outside.)
5. Challenge your friends to figure out how the wire got into the middle of the solid block of ice.

Sport mini-mystery: Why do cross-country skiers wax their skis?

It's not to make them slippery. In fact, it's just the opposite—it's to make them grip the snow. That's the technique of cross-country skiing: first, the right ski grips the snow while the left ski glides forward, then the left ski grips the snow while the right ski glides forward.

When you step down on a cross-country ski, the snow and the wax on the bottom of the ski actually lock together. The little points, or ''arms,'' on the snowflakes stick into the wax and hold the ski in place. This connection between the wax and the snow is just strong enough to provide a base from which to push yourself forward.

Different kinds of snowflakes require different kinds of wax. Newly fallen flakes are like the ones you see on Christmas cards—they have long, pointy arms that can grab onto a hard wax. But as snowflakes grow older, their arms grow shorter. Middle-aged snowflakes with their shorter, rounded arms require a soft wax. Eventually snowflakes have no arms at all. They can only grab a wax so soft and gooey it comes packaged in a squeeze tube, like toothpaste.

ARE you using up too much energy when you bicycle? You are if your tires don't have enough air in them. Here's an experiment to show you how to increase your pedal power — without using any more energy.

You'll need:
a bicycle pump
some chalk
a hill

1. Make sure your tires are inflated to the proper pressure (it's often printed on the side of the tire itself).
2. Walk your bike to the top of a hill, give yourself a little push — just enough to start the bike rolling — and coast down the hill.
3. When your bike has rolled to a stop, mark the spot with the chalk.
4. Walk your bike back to the top of the hill and let air out of your tires, so they're only about half-inflated.
5. Start off with the same gentle push as before and coast down the hill. Do you think you'll go as far?

How does it work?

All objects (including your bike tires) resist sliding, moving, or rolling across other objects (the road); this resistance is called *friction*. Friction increases with the amount of contact between the objects. So the less air in a tire, the more it flattens out against the ground, and the more friction there is between the tire and the road. This makes it harder for the tire to roll, and the bike slows more quickly when you coast.

Increased friction also makes you work harder to pedal your bike, so you'll save a lot of your energy by making sure that your bike tires are sufficiently inflated. You can help save fuel energy, too, by checking the tire pressure on your family car. The correct pressure for safety and efficiency is printed on a sticker, usually inside the car door.

EXT time you have to lift something heavy, try using an energy-saving ramp. Here's an experiment to show how a ramp can help you.

You'll need:
a thin rubber band
a rock about the size of your fist
a piece of string long enough to tie around the rock
a ruler
3 books

1. Wrap the string around the rock and tie the rubber band to it so that you can pull the rock.
2. Stack the books on top of one another and lean the ruler on top of them, as shown.
3. Use the rubber band to pull the rock up the ruler. Notice how far the rubber band stretches.
4. Remove the ruler and lift the rock up onto the books using the elastic. Does the rubber band stretch farther this time?

How does it work?
The longer the band gets, the more force you're using to move the rock from the ground to the top of the pile of books. It doesn't matter whether you use a ramp or lift the rock straight up, you're doing the same amount of work, but the length the rubber band stretches will show you the difference in the force needed to do that work. Now use a different length of ruler as a ramp and see what happens. When you use a ramp, its size depends on the size and weight of the object you are trying to move.

SCIENCE WHATS, HOWS & WHYS

HOW DO THINGS FLY?

BACK in the 11th century, a man called the Saracen of Constantinople decided to try to fly. He fitted wooden slats into a flowing robe and, flapping these makeshift wings, leapt from a high tower. His flight was a short one. It ended with a "splat!" on the ground below.

As time went on, would-be birdmen from all over Europe continued "hang gliding" off castles and cathedrals. They all contacted the ground with the same rude jolt.

A few inventors had some success with hang gliders in the 19th century. But it wasn't really until the 1960s that hang gliding caught on as a safe and popular sport.

Hang gliders work the same way as all other flying things. They put air to work to help them fly. How? When a hang glider throws himself off a cliff, air starts flowing around the glider's wing. The faster air moves, the lower the air pressure. The curved shape of the wing makes the air move faster over the top of the wing than over the bottom. This makes the air pressure lower over the top of the wing than under it. The result is lift.

Can you make a piece of paper *lift* without touching it? If you can, you'll have an idea of how *hang gliders* (and other aircraft) stay up.

You'll need:
a piece of paper

1. Hold one edge of the paper between your thumb and your index finger, letting the rest of the paper droop over your other fingers, as in the drawing.
2. Now bring your mouth close to your thumb and blow hard over the top of the paper. What happens? You've created an essential ingredient of flight, lift.

What's lift? Whenever an aircraft wing moves into the wind, it cuts the airflow in two. Instead of one *airstream*, there are now two, one flowing over the top of the wing, the other flowing under the wing. If the wing had been built with a curved top and a flat bottom, the airstream running over the top follows a different path than the airstream passing under the bottom. This creates a difference in air pressure between top and bottom of the wing and "lift" is the result.

By blowing over your piece of paper, you provided the airstream that lifted it.

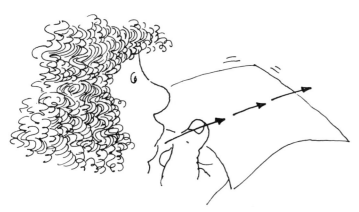

Playing the angles

Frisbees need a lift, too. That's why they're slightly curved on top, to break the airflow into different paths. But the curve on a frisbee isn't enough to take it far.

Your throw makes a difference.

Try throwing a frisbee parallel to the ground. Watch how high it goes and where it lands. Go back to your starting point and throw again, this time tilting the frisbee so the front edge is slightly higher than the back edge. Throw it with a tilt. What's different about its flight path? Can you find the angle of tilt that makes it go farthest?

AMAZING HOMEMADE AIRPLANES

TIRED of the same old paper airplane designs? Try these two unusual flying wonders.

Straw Plane

You'll need:

one strip of paper 1.5 cm × 9 cm (½ inch × 3½ inches) long

one strip of paper 2 cm × 12 cm (¾ inch × 4¾ inches) long

a regular-sized plastic straw

cellophane tape

1. Make a loop out of each strip of paper, overlapping the ends and taping them inside and outside the loop. The overlapped ends will form a pocket into which you can slip the straw.
2. Put one loop on each end of the straw by slipping the straw through the pockets you've made.
3. Experiment with the loops in different positions along the straw. Try it with the loops on the top and the bottom and take turns putting each loop at the front.

How does it work?

Paper airplanes — even the odd looking one you've just made — fly using the same principles as real airplanes. When they're moving, the shape and angle of their wings cause the air to move faster over the wing than under it. This reduces the pressure of the air above the wing, increases the pressure underneath the wing, and the plane is held up by the difference.

A real airplane must race down the runway to get the air moving fast enough past the wings to create enough difference in air pressure to lift it, and then must stay above a minimum speed while in the air. A helicopter, on the other hand, moves just its wings — the whirling rotors. This forces the air past them at a speed that's enough to lift it off the ground, or slow its descent.

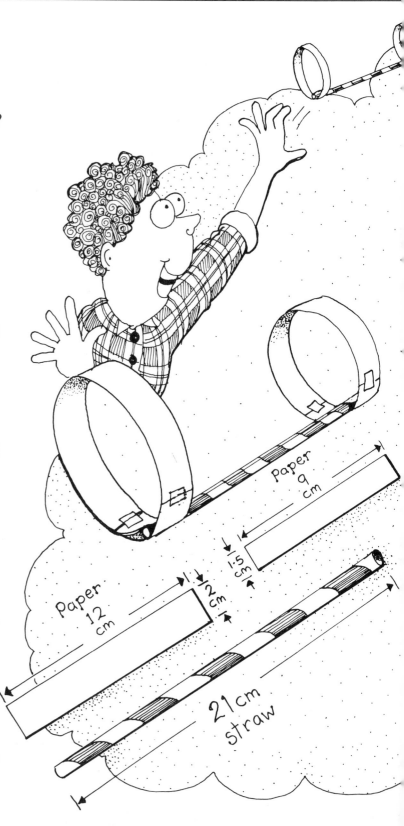

Paper 9 cm

1.5 cm

Paper 12 cm

2 cm

21 cm straw

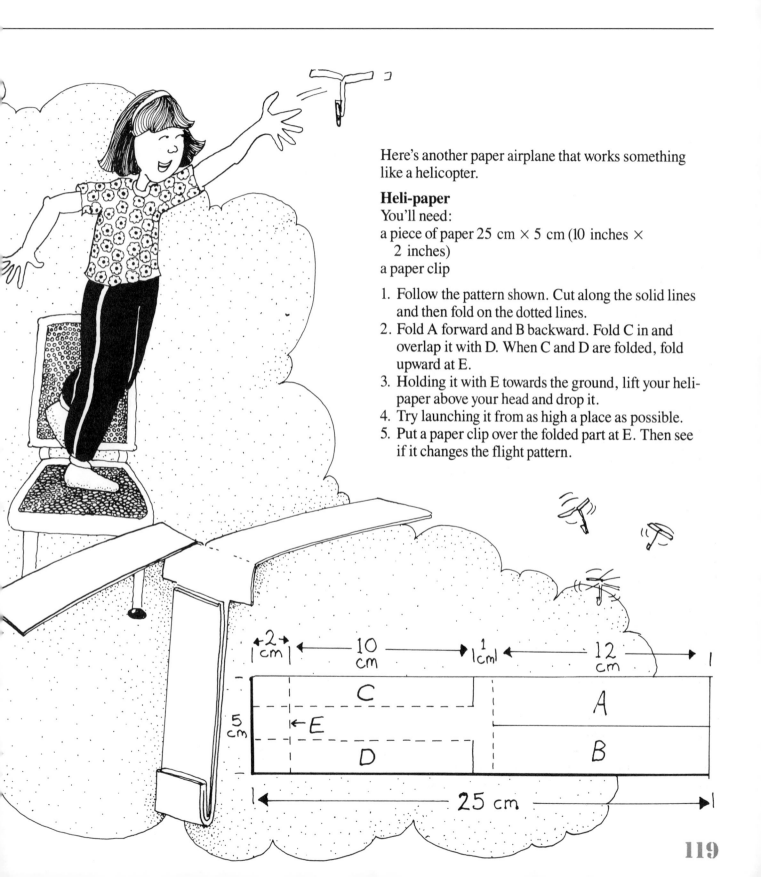

Here's another paper airplane that works something like a helicopter.

Heli-paper
You'll need:
a piece of paper 25 cm × 5 cm (10 inches × 2 inches)
a paper clip

1. Follow the pattern shown. Cut along the solid lines and then fold on the dotted lines.
2. Fold A forward and B backward. Fold C in and overlap it with D. When C and D are folded, fold upward at E.
3. Holding it with E towards the ground, lift your heli-paper above your head and drop it.
4. Try launching it from as high a place as possible.
5. Put a paper clip over the folded part at E. Then see if it changes the flight pattern.

WHY DO BALLS BOUNCE?

I N the major sports leagues, it's not just the athletes who have to stay in top condition. Sports equipment must be kept in good shape, too, or risk being thrown out of the game.

How do you check if a ball is in good shape? By the way it bounces back!

In every major ball sport, there are standards for measuring a ball's bounciness. And balls have to meet those standards rigidly. . .er, bouncily. Why? Think about basketball for example. If every ball had a different bounce, the play would change every time a new ball was used. Imagine dribbling a basketball with the bounciness of a superball then switching to a basketball that bounced like a baseball. The same goes for all other ball sports.

Balls bounce because when they hit the floor they are flattened out. Things made of rubber tend to return to their original shape after they've been squashed, and a ball is no exception. It rebounds from the floor as it restores itself to its usual round shape. The bounciness tells you how quickly the ball is restoring itself to its former roundness. When a ball can no longer restore itself well, it's bounced from the game. In general, a ball lasts one year in a major sports league.

What kind of standards do balls have to meet?

When dropped from a height of 182.9 cm (72″), a basketball must rebound to a height of between 125.5 and 137 cm (49 -54″).

When dropped from a height of 254 cm (100″), a volleyball or soccer ball must rebound to a height of between 152.4 and 165.1 cm (60-65″). These figures are set out by the sports leagues. Balls for home use are made less expensively than those made for the professional leagues, so their bounciness will be different.

How bouncy are the balls in your house? Check them out with this test.

You'll need:
a variety of balls—for example, a rubber ball, superball, tennis ball, basketball, volleyball, soccer ball
a metrestick (yardstick)
a pencil or felt pen
a hard floor
some notepaper

1. Hold the first ball at the top of the metrestick and drop it.
2. Mark the measuring stick at the highest point of the ball's bounce. (It may take a couple of tries until you get practised at noticing where the top of the bounce is.) Which ball bounces highest? Note your results.
3. Try the test again on different surfaces. Which produces more bounce, a vinyl floor or a wood floor? How about a fresh-cut lawn, concrete sidewalk, mattress or gravel road? Do different surfaces affect the bounce ranking of your ball collection?

Thermo-Bounce

A strange argument raged during the Chicago White Sox/Detroit Tigers weekend baseball series in Chicago in July 1965. The Tigers accused the Sox of illegally refrigerating the baseballs. They said that was why only 17 runs had been scored in five games.

"Ridiculous!" answered the Chicago team, pitching an accusation in return. They said that during the previous five games in Detroit, the balls played as though they'd been cooked! How else to explain the 59 runs scored, including 19 home runs!

Were these players crazy? Or do hot balls really have more bounce than normal, while cold balls have less?

You be the umpire. We'll probably never know whether the two teams really did tamper with the balls. But you can find out if there was a basis for all their name-calling.

You'll need:
the same balls and equipment you used for your bounce test, and the results of your testing
a freezer
an oven

1. Chill the balls in a freezer for one hour.
2. Bring them out one at a time and test the bounciness of each ball as soon as you take it from the freezer. Note the results.
3. Wait a few hours to make sure the balls have thoroughly thawed, then sit them on a rack or cookie sheet and pop them in an oven at 105° C (225° F) for 15 minutes. Make sure none of the balls is close to the oven elements.

4. Give them the one-at-a-time drop test again and note the results.

Were the baseball teams right? Could they really cook the results by cooking the balls?

AS THE BALL TURNS

HAVE you ever seen a seal balance a ball on its nose? It looks easy. . .until you try it yourself. If your nose knows it isn't having a ball, try to balance the ball on your finger, the way a basketball player does. Sit the ball there and it falls off. But twirl it the way the basketball player (or the seal) does, and you can keep it perched on your finger for much longer.

The secret is all in the spin. The faster the spin, the better the ball behaves.

Lots of ball sports use spinning balls. Football players spin the ball for greater control as they throw passes. A well-thrown short pass is sometimes called a "bullet pass," and for good reason. Bullets also spin. A rifle barrel has spiral grooves carved along the inside of its barrel that put a spin on the bullet as it passes through.

What happens without the spin? Try throwing a football without a spin. The result is a quarterback's nightmare. Tumbling head over heels, the ball will veer off course and plop to the ground in a hurry.

Frisbees spin as they travel, too. How far will a frisbee go without the spin?

Spinning footballs, bullets and frisbees all benefit from gyroscopic stability. This is the tendency for a spinning object to keep its axis (the centre around which it's turning—think of the hub or axle of a bike wheel) pointed in a constant direction.

Does that mean a spinning football should fly straight to its target? Not really. As the ball travels through the air, it loses some of its gyroscopic stability to air resistance. This creates a "wobble," called precession. The football no longer points straight ahead. Instead, its ends turn like a corkscrew, drawing small circles in the air as it moves.

Any spinning object that is not perfectly balanced will precess—even our own Earth. The Earth is spinning around its own axis, making one revolution every 24 hours. The Earth's spin is not perfect, however, due to the gravitational pull of the Sun and Moon. So the Earth has a wobble. A very slow wobble. Scientists estimate that it takes about 26 000 years for the Earth to precess just once.

Turn a magarine top into a margarine top

You'll need:

a couple of ballpoint pens

a couple of plastic lids (e.g., from margarine and yoghurt containers)

a large pad of paper

1. Punch the ballpoint of a pen through the centre of the margarine lid so that the tip of the pen pokes a couple of centimetres (half an inch or so) through the other side.
2. Press the ballpoint against the paper. Twirl the end of the pen in your fingers or between your palms, as if you were twirling a top, then let go.
3. Watch it draw. (If the ballpoint pen doesn't work after several tries, use a sharp felt-tipped pen instead.)

How can you get your pen top to draw patterns? By allowing it to precess across the paper. A tilted top will precess as gravity tries to pull it over. Gradually, you'll see the loops increase. The large loops are precession drawings.

Want to add small loops for prettier patterns? Try adding bits of Plasticine to one edge of the lid. You may find small loops in your drawing even without the added Plasticine—that's because the pen is a little off-centre in the lid.

Use other lids and pens for home-made tops of different sizes. Try poking the pen well off-centre through the lid and see what the top draws.

WHY DO CURVE BALLS CURVE?

 AVE you ever seen a ball break in mid-air? It happens all the time, or haven't you noticed?

"Break" is the word that baseball pitchers use to describe those throws that curve in flight—they *break* away from their original path. From a batter's point of view, a curve ball will seem to come straight in and then drop suddenly, as if it had rolled off the edge of a table.

To make a ball break, you have to spin it when you throw or hit it. Why does a spin put a curve on a ball? A ball moving through the air is surrounded by a thin layer of air which "sticks" to the ball as it flows around it. (The stitches on a baseball and the fuzz on a tennis ball help to grab hold of this layer of air.) On a ball without a spin, this layer of air moves around the ball and then separates from it at the back to form a wake of turbulent air.

On a ball with a top spin, however, the turning motion of the ball pulls the air on the bottom around to the back and then gives it an extra shove, throwing the wake upwards. The effect of this is to push the ball towards the ground.

Similarly, the wake on a ball with a back spin will be thrown downwards, keeping the ball from dropping as quickly (a back-spin curve is what creates a fastball). The wake on a ball with a side spin will be thrown to the side, pushing it in the opposite direction.

Being able to put a curve on a baseball (or a tennis ball) takes a strong arm, plenty of practice, proper coaching and a certain level of physical maturity. Many baseball coaches advise kids not to try putting a curve on a baseball until they're in their mid-teens.

But you don't need all of that to put a spin on a beach ball.

You'll need:
a beach ball

1. Hold the beach ball on your outstretched hand.
2. Bring your other hand up fast, the way you would if you were hitting a volleyball, but instead of hitting the ball right on, let the flat of your hand hit it on the side as you pass it. It's almost as if you were grazing the side of the ball, but hard.
3. Watch it curve!

Foam balls are also good for trying out a few curves. Grip the ball with your thumb and first two fingers. Throw, but just before you let go of the ball, twist your hand slightly to one side to start it spinning. Start out with side spins which are easiest to throw, and then move on to a top-spinning ball. Try throwing it with a back spin against the floor. Which way does it bounce?

WHY DO GOLF BALLS HAVE DIMPLES?

A LONG time ago, golf balls were called featheries. You made one by stuffing boiled goose feathers inside a casing of untanned bull's hide. You then sewed the feather-stuffed leather shut, moulded it into a round shape and painted it white. When you hit it, you hoped the feathers would help it fly. And it did fly better than the previous type of golf ball, which was carved from boxwood.

The featheries flew for 150 years. Then, in the mid-1800s, a clergyman at St. Andrews University in Scotland fashioned a new type of golf ball out of gutta-percha, a rubbery substance from India.

Excited by his invention, the clergyman took his gutta-percha ball, nicknamed a "guttie," out to the course. His first hit was a failure. The guttie sank sharply back to earth after flying only a short distance. The clergyman didn't give up easily; he hit the ball again and again and eventually noticed that as his club pitted and scarred the guttie, it stayed airborne longer.

Soon, golf ball manufacturers were mass-producing the guttie with specially moulded craters, or "dimples," on its surface. The more dimples they added to a ball, the farther it sailed. Today, golf balls, which are made of rubber with a hard enamel coating, have more dimples than Shirley Temple.

Why are dimpled balls superior to smooth ones? The answer lies in the way the air flows around the ball as it moves.

As the ball moves, it drags along a very thin layer of air, called the boundary layer. On a smooth ball, the boundary layer breaks away before it gets completely around the ball, leaving a very large "wake" dragging behind the ball like a

boundary layer separates

delayed separation of boundary layer

parachute. This puts a brake on the ball's momentum and sends it into an early nosedive.

To get rid of that parachute, you have to make the boundary layer stick to the ball all the way around to the back. Dimples mix the boundary air with the next outer layer of faster-moving air, giving the boundary layer an extra push that carries it to the back of the ball. The wake behind a dimpled ball is much narrower, and the ball sails farther.

On average, dimpled balls travel about four times the distance of smooth ones.

Putting around

- Probably the most unusual golf game ever was played on the moon by Captain Alan Shepard in February 1971.

- Floyd Satterlee Rood played the longest golf game ever. He putted from the Atlantic coast to the Pacific coast of the United States during a game that lasted nearly 13 months.

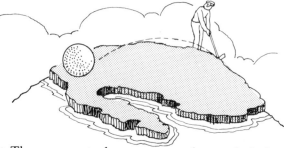

- The youngest player ever to shoot a hole in one, according to the *Guinness Book of World Records*, was Coby Orr of Littleton, Colorado. He was only five years old at the time.

WHY DON'T SPINNING SKATERS GET DIZZY?

TRICK question! Spinning skaters *do* get dizzy—but they use their eyes to keep from losing their balance. Which is a little odd because twirling skaters (and everyone else) get dizzy because of their ears.

Inside each of your ears, past where you can reach when you wash, are fluid-filled canals. In the canals are jelly-like capsules sprouting tiny hairs that are actually sensors that send messages to the brain. When your head turns, the fluid moves in the same direction, but lagging a little behind at the start. As it lags, it presses against the hairy capsules, triggering the hairs to transmit a message about the direction and speed of your movement.

After you've been spinning for a little while, the fluid catches up with the canal and you have to rely on messages from your eyes and your muscles to tell you that you're still turning. When you suddenly stop, you feel like you're still moving because the fluid in your inner ear hasn't stopped moving yet. You also feel as though you're moving in the opposite direction, because the still-moving fluid is pushing against the other side of the jelly capsule.

Now your brain is getting contradictory messages—your muscles say you've been going one way and you've stopped, while your ears say you're going the other way and you're still moving. Your eyes are no help because they still haven't focussed on anything. This confusion is what we call being dizzy.

How do spinning skaters use their eyes to keep from falling over from dizziness? With practice, skaters learn how to focus their eyes intently on a stationary object as soon as they stop spinning so their brain can sort out the mixed messages more quickly.

You can see the way the fluid in your ear canals lags behind the movement of your head.

You'll need:
breakfast—some milk and floating cereal (o-shaped oats are good) in a bowl

1. Gently spin the bowl in one direction. Watch the cereal to see when the milk it's floating on starts moving.
2. Stop the bowl. Watch which way the cereal goes. (Over the edge doesn't count.)
3. Eat the cereal.

HOW CAN A BOARD BE BROKEN WITH A BARE HAND?

ID you ever get really angry and smash your hand down on a table? Hurts, doesn't it? And you didn't even get the satisfaction of denting the table!

If all you could manage was a sore hand, a solid table and a stupid look, how do karate experts break boards without breaking their hands?

Part of the secret lies in the fact that the board bends when the hand comes down on it. As the board bends, its upper half compresses, or squeezes together, while its lower half experiences tension, a kind of stretching apart. As it stretches, the lower half of the board starts to crack. The crack quickly spreads upward and the board breaks in two. If you look at the way boards are set up for this demonstration, you'll notice they are usually supported only at the ends, which gives them lots of room to bend.

Another part of the secret lies in the karate expert's aim and speed. The hand is moving at full speed when it hits the board because it's aimed at a point below the surface.

Why doesn't the hand break, too? Because some of the stress is absorbed by the skin and muscles lying between the bones and the wood. Also, some of the force is transmitted to other parts of the body. Karate experts are careful to hold their hand in certain positions, called "knife hand" or "hammer fist," and make contact only with the portion that can absorb the stress best.

Scientists estimate that in a karate "chop," the human hand can apply nearly six times the force it takes to break a pine board and nearly a third more force than is needed to break a concrete block.

So your hands are a lot tougher than you thought they were. But don't assume that this makes you an instant expert. A karate student studies and practises for years before she dares to bring down her powerful knife hand or hammer fist on a block of wood or slab of concrete. Doing this without instruction and training can be very dangerous.

WHAT MAKES POPCORN POP?

POPCORN has been around for a long time, even before the movies. The Incas used it for decoration hundreds of years ago, and the Native People of North America introduced the Pilgrims to it at the first Thanksgiving dinner ever held.

One of the nicest things about popcorn is that you can eat as much as you want of it and all it'll spoil is your appetite. A mug full of plain popcorn has just a bit of protein and fat, some fibre that you need in your diet and only 25 calories.

If you've popped popcorn, though, you've probably noticed that some batches come out fluffier and softer than others. Why? The secret's inside the kernel.

If you carefully cut a kernel of popping corn in half, you would see that it's very tightly packed with softer, slightly moist material. The kernel is really the seed of a new corn plant, and the moisture sealed inside helps keep it alive until conditions are right for sprouting. The moisture is what makes the corn pop.

If the kernel is heated very quickly, the moisture vaporizes into steam and expands rapidly, exerting enough pressure to burst the kernel open. When the tight jacket of the kernel bursts, the material inside expands, rather like a released jack-in-the-box springing to its full height.

How important is that internal drop of water for producing good popcorn? Here's an experiment you can munch through.

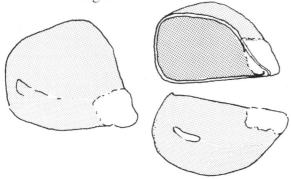

The popcorn test

You'll need:
about 125 mL (½ c) fresh popping corn
a cookie sheet
a ruler

1. Measure out 50 mL (¼ c) of kernels of corn and count them. Count out another batch with the same number of kernels.
2. Preheat the oven to 100° C (200° F). Spread one batch of corn kernels out on the cookie sheet and put them in the oven for 90 minutes.
3. While they're heating, pop the other batch of kernels. Count the number of kernels that **don't** pop, then measure the length of ten of the popped ones. Choose the ten at random—just stick your hand into the bowl and take a bunch. Add up the measurements and divide by ten to find their average size. Write down your findings so you don't forget them.
4. Keep your notes and eat the popcorn.
5. After 90 minutes, ask an adult to help you remove the heated kernels from the oven. Let them cool. Then pop them the same way as the first batch. Again, count the unpopped kernels and measure ten of the ones that pop. Eat a kernel or two and compare with the first batch.
6. Eat the rest and try to figure out what caused the difference between the two batches of popcorn. (Clue: water evaporates in heat.)

What do you think would happen if you soaked stale popping corn in water before popping it?

WHY ARE HOT DRINKS SO HOT AT FIRST?

W HY do the first few sips of cocoa always seem hotter than the later ones? Does your mouth get used to the heat? Does the drink cool off as you sip it? To solve the mystery, try this.

You'll need:
a piece of string about 30 cm (1 foot) long
a small bottle
a large jar
food colouring

1. Tie the string around the neck of the small bottle.
2. Fill the large jar with cold water.
3. Fill the small bottle with hot water and quickly stir in enough food colouring to make a strong colour.
4. Use the string to gently lower the small bottle into the large one filled with cold water. Don't let the small bottle tip. As the bottle drops, it will release a coloured fountain of hot water. Even after the bottle is settled on the bottom of the jar, coloured water will rise out of it. Soon all the coloured water will be floating at the top of the jar.

How does it work?
Water expands and rises when it's heated. This is what makes the hot, coloured water rise to the surface. It's also the reason why the top layer of cocoa is hotter than the rest.

Do you think this holds true for cold drinks, too? Can you think of a way to find out if cold drinks are colder on the bottom?

Here's a hint: try using an ice cube made of vegetable-dyed water.

132

HOW DOES SOUND TRAVEL?

ID you ever wonder how sound travels? Here's a neat experiment that lets you see sounds on the move.

You'll need:
2 glasses about the same size and shape
a pencil
a piece of fine wire long enough to rest on the rim of one glass, as shown

1. Half fill the two glasses with water.
2. Tap the first glass with a pencil. You'll hear a musical note. Try to produce the same note on the second glass. You'll have to add or subtract water to get the second glass to make the same note.
3. Set the two glasses about 10 to 12 cm (4 to 5 inches) apart and rest the fine wire across the top of the one farthest from you.
4. Now tap the nearest glass and you will see the wire move slightly on the other one!

How does it work?
When you tap the first glass with a pencil, you start it vibrating. Although the vibrations are too small to be seen, they're strong enough to push the air forward in waves, like a stone thrown in water pushes out ripples. These sound waves cause similar vibrations in the other glass. It's these vibrations in the second glass that make the wire move. If you keep tapping the first glass, you can make the wire move to the edge of the second glass and it will eventually fall off.

Hear, hear!
Your ear picks up vibrations much like the wire does. Inside your ear is a sensitive piece of tissue called an eardrum. It vibrates when sound waves hit it. These vibrations are transmitted to your brain via your middle and inner ear. There the vibrations are "decoded" into sounds.

ERE'S an unusual chance to see a sound.

You'll need:
a balloon
scissors
an orange juice or soup can with both
   ends removed
rubber bands
tape
glue
a tiny piece of mirror about 0.5 cm (½ inch) square
a flashlight

1. Cut the neck off the balloon and stretch the remaining part tightly over one end of the can. Hold the balloon in place with rubber bands and tape the edge of the balloon to the can to keep it from slipping.
2. Glue the piece of mirror (face out) to the stretched balloon, about a third of the way in from the edge of the can.
3. Now shine the flashlight onto the mirror at an angle, so that you can see a bright spot from the mirror reflected on the wall. If you don't have a plain wall to aim the spot at, use a piece of white cardboard as a screen.
4. Hold the can very still (or set it on a table, braced so it won't roll) and sing or shout into the open end of the tin. Watch the spot of light on the wall. Why does it vibrate quickly back and forth?

How does it work?
Sound is made by vibrations. When you sing or shout, the air rushing from your lungs passes through your vocal cords and makes them vibrate, producing pressure waves that travel through the air, like ripples in water. When these waves hit the stretched balloon, they make it vibrate. This, in turn, starts both the mirror and the light reflecting from it, vibrating.

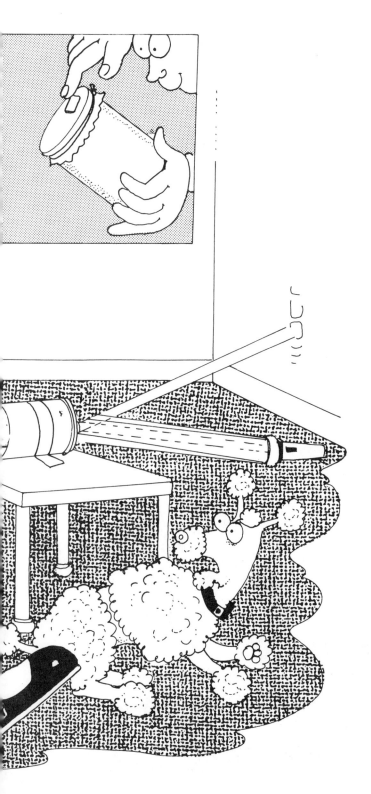

Your eardrum is a stretched membrane something like the balloon. When pressure waves strike the eardrum, it vibrates and your brain interprets those vibrations as sounds.

Human Voice vs Tape Voice
Remember how surprised you were when you heard your voice on a tape recorder for the first time? What makes it sound different? When you hear your voice on tape, you're hearing it after the sound waves have travelled through air. But usually you hear your voice through the bones of your head, and it sounds different. The way you sound on tape is actually closer to how others hear you.

Hearing Through Your Teeth
Find out what good "sound conductors" your head bones are.

You'll need:
a fork
a spoon

Hit the tines of the fork with the spoon and listen to the note produced by the vibrating fork. As soon as the sound fades, put the end of the fork handle between your teeth and bite firmly on it.

RUBBER SOLE

AS the idea of competition ever given you cold feet? Well, this experiment will, too.

You'll need:
a pair of sneakers
a plastic bag
a freezer

1. Put your sneakers on and walk around in them. Rub your feet along the ground. Notice how much you slide. Bounce up and down.
2. Close your sneakers in a plastic bag and put them in the freezer. Make sure the plastic bag is a fairly thick one or you'll run the risk of having food that tastes like feet. Leave them there for 24 hours.
3. Put the sneakers on (they may be stiff so be careful not to tear them) and try your running, sliding and bouncing experiments again.

Why do frozen sneakers slide and bounce differently than warm ones?

Normally, there's a lot of friction between your sneaker soles and the ground. That's what allows you to get a good grip when you walk or run. Friction always occurs wherever two objects rub against each other. You can see why if you look at any object under a microscope. No matter how smooth the surface of that object may look to the naked eye, it will appear very bumpy or jagged under the microscope. Whenever two objects are pressed together, their uneven surfaces ''interlock,'' like pieces of a jigsaw puzzle fitting together.

Sneakers give you a better grip on the ground because rubber is a soft material. It moulds itself more to the ground, providing more friction. Hard surfaces, such as the soles of leather shoes, make contact with the ground in only a few places.

When you freeze your sneakers, their rubber soles become harder. They no longer make as much contact with the ground so you slide where normally you'd grip.

In many sports, athletes want to increase friction to prevent sliding. Have you ever seen baseball pitchers rubbing a small bag between their hands? They're putting rosin (pronounced ''rozzin'') on their hands to increase friction and improve their grip on the ball. Pole vaulters use sticky adhesive tape on the pole or rosin on their hands to achieve a similar result. The covering on a ping-pong paddle improves the ''grip'' between the paddle and the ball, so you can give spin to the ball.

Mountain climbers use pressure to increase friction. A rock climber knows that by leaning well away from the rock face, he can thrust more firmly against the surface of the rock. This helps to hold the rock and soles of his boots more tightly together, and reduces the likelihood of slipping.

Of course, not all sports aim to increase the ''grip'' between two surfaces. Take bowling, for example. The best way to steer a bowling ball for a strike is to give it a spin so that it curves at the far end of the lane and scoots in behind the head pin.

Unfortunately, because bowling lanes are so long, a ball with a spin on it will quickly veer off into the gutter. That's why the first 10 m (30 feet) or so of a bowling lane is always covered with a light coating of oil. As the bowling ball rumbles over this oil slick, it spins but it doesn't curve. Only when the oil slick thins out and the ball makes contact with the wood surface of the lane does it finally start to swerve. Friction between the ball and the wood acts as a sideways force, making the spinning ball curve sideways and, with luck, into position for a strike.

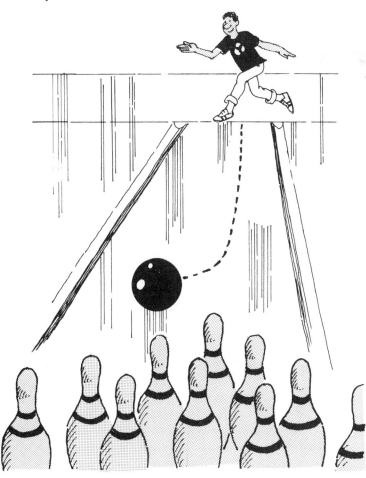

HOW DO HELMETS PROTECT YOUR HEAD?

WHEN is a sheet like a football helmet?

You'll need:
an egg
a sheet
two friends

1. Ask your friends to hold the sheet as in the drawing.
2. Stand back from the sheet and throw the egg at it. Throw the egg as hard as you can. What happens?

Why didn't the egg break? Because the sheet behaved like a football helmet. When a football player wearing a helmet is struck on the head, the helmet's padding absorbs and spreads out the shock. Your sheet did the same thing when the egg hit it. Compare this (but only in your imagination!) with what happens when you throw an egg against a wall, where the egg's shell has to take the full force of the impact. Now imagine that the egg is your head.

When you do that, it seems that only a dodo would ever fail to wear a helmet.

The same goes for face protectors. Puck sandwiches taste terrible, though that never used to stop hockey goal-tenders from dining on them regularly. And talk about fast food: these high-speed lunches would be delivered at up to 200 km/h (about 120 mph).

Eventually, goalies got smart and started wearing masks. Goalie Gerry Cheevers of the Boston Bruins used to decorate his mask with drawings of the stitches that he would have received if he had gone barefaced. The mask had more stitch marks on it than Frankenstein!

Though wearing proper protective equipment might seem like a common-sense idea, it's still just catching on. The batting helmets that baseball players wear can only protect them from fastballs moving less than 95 km/h (60 mph). And yet, most fastballs in the major leagues travel much faster than that. Many bicycle racers still don't wear helmets, even though they travel at speeds that could cause them serious head injuries if they fell.

What makes a good helmet? For starters, helmets should have an outer shell that stops penetration by sharp objects, such as hockey sticks or ski poles. So far, fibreglass has proven to be the most puncture-proof material. Also, chin straps on a helmet must be flexible enough to resist snapping when the helmet is struck. Finally, the helmet should have a liner like the sole of a running shoe, capable of absorbing or slowing down the strongest shocks.

Helmets have to match the sport they're used for. Contact sports, such as football and hockey, require helmets with padding that can bounce back after every blow, like a sponge. Crash helmets worn by racing car drivers, motorcyclists and downhill skiers have a different kind of lining, like styrofoam, which can absorb more energy but crushes on impact. After one strong blow, the helmet must be retired.

How do helmet makers know how much shock a helmet will absorb? By dropping it on its head. An artificial head, of course. The artificial head, wearing its helmet, is dropped from a height of about 3 m (3 yards) onto a padded iron block. Inside the head is a small instrument that records its speed during the fall and also how suddenly the head comes to a stop when it hits the block. A good helmet will absorb enough of the impact to let the head inside slow down before hitting.

This is important because the human brain is suspended in fluid inside the skull. Whenever the head is struck, the brain moves through this fluid and hits its hard casing. If the jolt is severe, the brain's nervous tissue and blood vessels may be badly damaged.

Make a Helmet for an Egg
Conduct your own helmet test, but with an egg instead of a head inside.

You'll need:
a couple of eggs
a chair
a frying pan

1. Make a helmet for the egg. What makes a good helmet for an egg? That's for you to find out. You might want to wrap the egg in cotton batting, or maybe some newspaper. Or both. How about tying your helmet to a homemade parachute? The possibilities are endless.

2. Stand on a chair, hold the helmeted egg as high as you can and drop it into a frying pan sitting on the floor.
3. Make an omelette out of the non-survivors.

THINGS TO MAKE

ERE'S a way you can see around corners or over the heads in a crowd. You just have to bend light. A job for Superman? No, you can do it yourself with this periscope.

You'll need:
scissors
a clean, empty milk carton
two pocket-sized mirrors
tape

1. Cut a hole in one side of the carton, near the top, and a similar hole in the opposite side, the same distance from the bottom.
2. Tape the two mirrors inside the box, facing one another as shown, making sure they're parallel to one another and slant across the box at a 45° angle.

3. When you have the mirrors secured inside, tape the top of the carton shut.
4. Take your periscope to a corner and hold it so just one hole is sticking out. Look through the other hole and you'll be able to see around the corner.

How does it work?
Light always bounces off a mirror at the same angle at which it hits. If it hits the mirror at 45°, it will reflect at 45°, enabling it to make the 90° turn around the corner. You can test this by shining a flashlight into the hole where you would look. If your mirrors are correctly angled, the light will shine out the other hole. Similarly, light reflecting off an object you're looking at will bounce off each mirror and into your spying eye.

SOME things are too small to see no matter how closely you look at them. That's why people invented magnifying glasses and microscopes — to make things appear bigger. Make your own version of a microscope and see what's hidden from view.

You'll need:
scissors
an old plastic pail
clear plastic wrap
water
string, tape, or a thick rubber band

1. Cut two or three fist-sized holes in the side of the pail, near the bottom.
2. Stretch the plastic wrap loosely across the top of the pail and fasten it securely around the side with the string, tape, or rubber band (or use all three together).
3. Pour water into the hollow formed by the plastic wrap until it is filled.
4. In a brightly lit room, put the object you're studying into the pail, through one of the holes.
5. Look down through the water into the pail. Move the object closer towards you and farther away until you've found the point where the object appears largest. Now find the point where the object is in the sharpest focus. Are they the same point?
6. Try to find the designer's initials on the back of Canadian pennies, quarters, and nickels. (Here's a clue for finding it on the quarter: look near the edge just in front of the caribou's chest.)

How does it work?
A lens bends light both as the light enters and again as it leaves. The material the lens is made of determines the angle at which the light bends. In this case, you've made a water lens. Reflected light spreading out from the object you're looking at hits the lens and is bent back to your eye (see the diagram). Your eye sees the light as though it came on a straight line from the object (the dotted lines in the diagram), and it appears as though you're looking at a much larger object a comfortable distance away.

Other ways of seeing
When scientists want to see something as tiny as germs, they use light microscopes with specially shaped and highly polished lenses. They also use electron microscopes which send beams of electrons through objects to produce pictures of things almost as small as atoms.

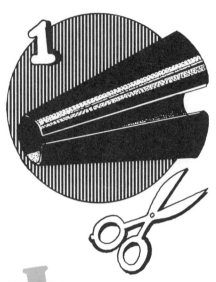

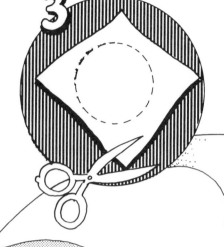

F you darkened a room and drilled a small hole through one outside wall, the light coming through that hole on a sunny day would form a dim, upside-down image on the far wall. If you fastened a large enough sheet of photographic paper to the wall and left it there long enough, you'd get a photograph of the scene outside.

This may sound farfetched, but it's much the way the first photograph was made in 1826 by a French physicist named Nicephore Niepce, using a device called a camera obscura, which means "dark chamber."

Here's a way to make a small version of the camera obscura.

You'll need:
black construction paper
wax paper or tracing paper
an empty, frozen orange juice can
tape

1. Roll the construction paper into a cone and trim the wide end until it just fits inside the can opening.
2. Tape or glue the cone to keep it in shape.
3. From the wax paper or tracing paper, cut a circle the same size as the wide end of your paper cone.

144

4. Tape your cut circle to the wide end of the cone. That's your viewing screen.
5. Make a pinhole in the closed end of the juice can and slide the paper cone screen into the open end.
6. Point the pinhole at a bright light or sunlit scene and look through the cone. You'll see an image projected upside down on the screen.
7. Slide the cone in and out of the can and the image will get larger and smaller.
8. Make a few more pinholes in the can. How many images can you see in the camera?

Why is the image always upside down?
Light usually travels in a straight line. If you had a flashlight and shone it through a hole from different angles, you'd see that light coming from a low angle strikes high on the surface behind the hole; light from above would strike low behind the hole. When you get an image through the aperture (hole) of the camera, light reflecting off the top of the object you're looking at strikes the bottom of your screen inside the camera. Light from the bottom of the object strikes the top of the screen. This explains why the image is formed upside down.

Do you have a favourite picture or photograph that you'd like to copy? Perhaps you'd like to make it larger or smaller than the original. Here's a bright way to do it.

You'll need:
a picture to copy (a clear, simple one is best to start with)
a 20 cm × 25 cm (8 inch × 10 inch) piece of glass (the glass from an old picture frame is good)
a piece of white paper
a pencil
a desk lamp

1. Put the picture and the piece of white paper side by side on a table.
2. Place the lamp beside the picture and shine the light directly on it. Hold the glass upright between the blank paper and the picture.
3. From the picture side, look through the glass and you'll see an image of the picture on the blank sheet. You may have to move your head until you find the best viewing spot for the image.
4. Hold the glass and your head steady and you can trace the image on the paper.

How does it work?

How can you see the picture on the paper when it isn't really there? Light shines on the picture and is reflected from it. Most of it just travels away in straight lines in all directions, but some of it bounces off the glass and into your eye.

When this reflected light enters your eyes, you see the picture as though it were on the paper. That's why moving your head can make the picture appear larger, or smaller, or make it disappear altogether.

What you've made is a simple version of the camera lucida, a device invented in 1807. It has often been used by both artists and scientists to enlarge or reduce drawings.

MAKING BUTTER

o you like to spread coalesced fat droplets on your bread? If you do, you can make some sandwiches with the results of this experiment.

You'll need:
300 mL (½ pint) whipping cream
a small glass jar with a tight cover

1. Take the cream out of the refrigerator and let it stand for about 10 minutes so that it warms up slightly.
2. Pour the cream into the jar until the jar is one-third full.
3. Screw on the lid and make sure it doesn't leak.
4. Hold the jar in one hand and shake it in a figure-eight motion. (You'll have to keep shaking it for about 20 minutes, so it might be a good idea to have a helper available to take over in case your arm gets tired.)
5. Watch the cream change form. It will become foamy and almost look like it's whipping, but after a while, very tiny granules of butter will start to form.
6. When the granules are the size of apple seeds, stop shaking.
7. Carefully drain off the liquid — it's buttermilk and very good to drink.
8. Wash the butter granules in cold water to rinse off any remaining buttermilk.
9. Put the butter granules in a plastic or wooden dish and pack them together with a wooden spoon. If you like salty butter, add a little salt and squish it into the butter with your wooden spoon. Make sure it's worked in evenly.
10. Form your butter into any shape you like, then put it into the refrigerator to harden.

How does it work?
Cream is very tiny fat droplets permanently floating in water. If enough of those droplets can be forced together, they'll form globules of butter and separate from the water. This is called coalescing.

Mellow Yellow
You might notice that your butter is darker or lighter than the butter you usually get in the store. That's because the colour of pure butter depends on the kinds of cows the milk came from and what they ate. But when people buy butter, they expect it to be a uniform golden colour, so dairies usually dye it with food colouring.

I SCREAM, YOU SCREAM, WE ALL SCREAM FOR ICE CREAM

YOU may have heard that Marco Polo brought ice cream back to Europe when he went to China in 1295. Well, he didn't. He ate it all on the way. Luckily, though, Marco did bring back the recipe. That original recipe didn't have cream in it. It was a water ice, made with fruit juice, sugar and water, the same way ices are made today. Cream didn't get into the recipe until 300 years later in France.

You can guess some of the major ingredients in ice cream—cream, milk, sugar, flavouring—but you'd probably never think of one of the most important ones—plain, unflavoured, uncoloured *air*.

Air is stirred into ice cream as it freezes. Without air, eating ice cream would be like chewing milky ice cubes. But you can have too much of a good thing. The more air ice cream has, the fluffier and warmer it seems (warmer because it contains less of the ice and icy liquid that make you feel the coldness). Some ice creams, usually the cheaper varieties, have as much air in them as all the other ingredients put together.

For most of its history, ice cream was home made in a bucket or other container and the stirring was done by hand. You can try stirring up a batch yourself.

Homemade ice cream

You'll need:
500 mL (2 c) cold 18% cream
125 mL (½ c) white sugar
2 mL (½ tsp) vanilla
plastic jug or similar container
1 dixie cup, 150 mL (4 oz)
1 styrofoam cup, 300-350 mL (8-10 oz)
clean snow or finely crushed ice
60 mL (4 Tbsp) table salt or coarse salt
2 stir sticks
thermometer that can measure below freezing
   (optional)

1. Mix the cream, sugar and vanilla together in the jug.
2. Pour some cream mixture into the dixie cup, filling it half to three-quarters full. Keep it cold.
3. Fill the styrofoam cup about one-third full with snow or ice. If you have a thermometer, measure the temperature of the ice.
4. Add about 45-60 mL (3 - 4 Tbsp) of salt to the ice. Stir. (Mark the stir stick you use so you won't mistakenly use it in the ice cream mix.) Measure the temperature of the ice again.
5. Make a hole in the icy slush big enough for the dixie cup and sit the cup in it so that ice comes up around the sides but doesn't get into the mixture.
6. Using the clean stir stick, stir the ice cream mixture slowly, scraping the newly formed crystals from the bottom and sides of the cup and stopping from time to time to let the ice cream solidify. You may have to stir on and off for 20-30 minutes until the ice cream is ready to eat—icy and only slightly soft. If you want to try other flavours, add a little chocolate syrup or other flavouring to the ice cream when it's at the slushy stage.

Why do you use salt water to freeze the ice cream?

Ice cream mix starts to freeze at -3° C (27° F), so your container has to be cooled below that. You could use solid ice from the freezer but the warm room air, the relative warmth of the ice cream mix and friction from the stirring would soon melt it around the inner container. Since ordinary water freezes at 0° C (32° F), even melted ice water is warmer than 0° C and too warm to freeze ice cream.

Salt water, though, has a lower freezing temperature than plain water. When you put salt and ice together you create a mix that can stay cold enough to freeze your ice cream.

Snow or crushed ice

Ice cream mixture

What's in that ice cream, anyway?

You might expect that the more you pay for a food, the more ingredients it would have. Ice cream is just the opposite.

Most premium-priced ice creams have the same ingredients you used in your experiment—cream, sugar, flavouring and air. Some of them may also add an egg, which not only makes a richer ice cream, but acts as an emulsifier, keeping the milk fat droplets separated and distributed evenly throughout the mix. This makes the ice cream smoother.

In cheaper ice cream, emulsifiers such as mono- and diglycerides substitute for eggs. And whey, a byproduct of cheesemaking, can substitute for some of the cream or milk. Artificial vanilla or other flavours can replace the real thing.

Then there are stabilizers, such as gelatin, carob, guar gum and carrageenan. These keep ice crystals from forming as ice cream warms and cools in the trip from manufacturer to your fridge and again every time you open the freezer door. All of these ingredients can change the flavour and texture of ice cream.

You can see what the stabilizers do to ice cream. All you need is some homemade ice cream (or a premium brand with just the basic ingredients) and some ice cream with as many stabilizers as possible. Spoon the same amount of each ice cream into separate dishes and let them melt. What are the differences? Which one would you rather slurp out of the bowl?

149

PROCESS YOUR OWN CHEESE

WHEN was the last time you had spoiled food for lunch? If you like cheese, probably not that long ago. Cheese was discovered centuries ago. According to legend, an Arab travelling across the desert decided to take some milk along with him. He poured it into a pouch he had made out of the stomach of a lamb.

He made the journey, but the milk didn't, at least not the way he had planned. When he arrived, he found not liquid milk, but chunky milk. He didn't know what had happened, but he was hungry, so he ate it. What a surprise! Spoiled milk tasted good!

The warm desert sun had changed the milk, with a little help from rennet, a substance found in the lamb's stomach where the milk was stored. Rennet helps young animals digest food. It combined with the milk and helped it to curdle. The rocking motion of the camel going up and down sand dunes churned the milk in the pouch. In three shakes of a lamb's stomach, they had cheese!

Famous Cheeses

If you're a mouse, cheese is cheese. But people tend to have favourites. Here's how three popular cheeses are made:

● People get wrinkles when they get older. Swiss cheese gets holes. During the aging process, special bacteria in the cheese give off a gas that makes big bubbles. Slice through a bubble and you get a piece of cheese with a hole. And you thought mice had been eating it!

● Cheddar cheese is cooked and drained like other cheeses and then it's "cheddared" or matted. That means the cheese is cut into slabs that are turned frequently and piled in layers to dry.

● If you put process cheese slices in a mousetrap, would you catch a process mouse? Actually, process cheese slices are made of real cheese mixed with milk powder and other ingredients, then heated and allowed to cool. The extra ingredients in process cheese help keep the oil from separating and also prevent the cheese from changing texture or going rubbery when it's heated. This process preserves the cheese and makes it cheaper to produce.

You can find out the difference between process and regular cheese with this experiment. Make two grilled cheese sandwiches, one with process cheese slices and the other with regular mild cheddar. Cut the finished sandwiches into pieces and mix them up, then try to pick out the process cheese pieces from the regular ones by their texture and appearance. Which one is chewier?

Make your own cheese

You'll need:
125 mL (½ c) homogenized milk
small saucepan
two large clear glasses (plastic or glass)
an eye dropper
liquid rennet (available at health food stores)
stir stick
piece of cheesecloth 15 cm (6 inches) square
   (you can use a J cloth or one like it)

1. Warm the milk in the saucepan over very low heat, stirring occasionally. Every couple of minutes, test the temperature of the milk by putting a drop of it on your inner wrist or arm. Test more frequently as the milk heats up. When the milk feels the same temperature as your skin, remove it from the heat.
2. Pour the milk into one of the glasses.
3. Using the dropper, add 4 or 5 drops of rennet to the milk.
4. Stir the milk briefly.
5. Stop stirring and wait about 20 minutes.
6. When you notice a clear, yellowish liquid, called whey, covering the surface of the mix, tip the glass. If the thickened milk, now called curds, breaks away from the sides of the glass, it's ready.
7. Place the cheesecloth over the mouth of the full glass. Hold the cheesecloth securely and turn the glass upside down over the empty glass. Let the liquid pour through into the empty glass. Now you have a cheesecloth full of curds and a glass full of whey. (Where's Miss Muffet when you need her?)
8. Hold the curds in the cheesecloth and squeeze the excess whey from them, letting it drip into the glass.
9. Open the cheesecloth. The small lump of white stuff is cheese. Taste it. If it's too bland, try adding a bit of salt. Most of the cheese you're used to eating has been aged to bring out the flavour.
10. Before you throw out your leftover whey, you might want to taste it. A great deal of whey is produced by the cheese-making industry. Most of it is used in animal feed, but some is also used as a milk substitute in many human foods. You often find it included in lower priced ice cream, for instance. How do you think it would affect the taste?

151

INSIDE STORY OF A CHOCOLATE BAR

RIDDLE: What grows on trees, is shaped like a melon and is full of beans?

Answer: Cacao pods, used to make the world's favourite treat—chocolate.

You find the yellow, red or green pods on the branches or trunks of cacao trees in warm countries like Brazil and Africa's Ivory Coast. After picking, you split the pods open with a sharp machete or knife. Inside, you find not chocolate but about 30 white beans.

You pile the beans on the ground, cover them with banana leaves and let them ferment for several days until they become brownish-red. Then you spread them out in the sun and dry them.

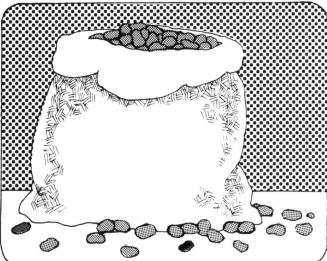

Bags of the dried beans are sent to chocolate factories. After cleaning and roasting, the shells are quite brittle and loose and the beans smell like chocolate. Next the beans are put through a machine that removes the shells and cracks the beans into small pieces, called nibs. Another machine grinds the nibs into a fine paste, called chocolate liquor.

If you just let chocolate liquor harden, you'll have baking chocolate. But there are two other things you can do with chocolate liquor—turn it into eating chocolate or separate it into its two ingredients, cocoa and cocoa butter.

When you mix chocolate liquor with extra cocoa butter and sugar, you get dark eating chocolate. If you add milk to the chocolate liquor, along with the extra cocoa butter and sugar, you get milk chocolate. If you don't use any chocolate liquor at all, but just mix cocoa butter with milk and sugar, you get "white chocolate," which isn't really chocolate at all because it doesn't contain any chocolate liquor.

Although this may sound quite simple, the actual amount of each ingredient is a closely guarded secret at a chocolate factory. No company wants anyone to know how their own special brand of chocolate is made.

A chocolate bar of your own

You'll need:

25 mL (2 Tbsp) powdered cocoa (the stuff you use to make cocoa from scratch)

25 mL (2 Tbsp) of sugar (table sugar is good, but fruit sugar produces a smoother result)

5 mL (1 tsp) of unsalted butter or vegetable shortening

a double boiler

wax paper

1. Put enough water in the bottom of the double boiler to just touch the top half when it's in place. Remove the top half and bring the water to a boil on the stove.

2. Turn off the heat and put the top half of the double boiler into place.

3. Put the cocoa, sugar and butter or shortening together into the top of the double boiler and stir until the mixture is smooth and the sugar is dissolved.

4. Spread the wax paper on a counter near the stove.

5. Ask an adult to remove the top of the double boiler and pour the chocolate mixture onto the wax paper.

Let it harden and taste.

If you made your chocolate with vegetable shortening, try another batch with butter. If you used butter, try vegetable shortening. Which do you prefer? You can experiment with the taste by slightly changing the proportions of cocoa, sugar and butter or shortening.

MAKING SUGAR CRYSTALS

ID you ever wonder where the sugar goes when you stir it into tea? It doesn't disappear. To prove it, here's an experiment that'll let you get the sugar out of a hot drink in beautiful crystal form.

You'll need:
a small saucepan
250 mL (1 cup) water
375 mL (1 ½ cups) sugar, or more
a drinking glass
a long pencil
a piece of cotton string

1. Ask an adult to boil the water in the saucepan. Turn off the heat, add the sugar and stir. As the sugar dissolves, add a little more and keep stirring until no more sugar will dissolve.
2. When the solution has cooled, pour it into the drinking glass.
3. Rub some sugar into the string so some crystals stick into it.
4. Tie one end of the string around the pencil and drop the other end into the solution. Rest the pencil on the rim of the glass.
5. Put the glass in a place where it will stay cool and undisturbed. (You mustn't touch it or lift it up!)
6. Leave it for a few days and watch what happens.
7. Eat the results.

How does it work?
To understand how you make the sugar reappear, you need to know what happens when the sugar dissolves. It doesn't really disappear, of course. It just breaks up into smaller and smaller pieces until you can no longer see it.

If you look at a sugar cube with a magnifying glass, you will see it is made up of lots of small crystals. These, in turn, are made up of tinier particles called molecules, the tiniest form of sugar that can exist. They are so tiny that you couldn't see them even with the most powerful microscope.

When you put your sugar in water, the sugar molecules break away from the crystal. This makes a sugar solution. The amount of sugar the water can hold depends on its temperature. Hot water can hold more than cold water.

As the solution cools, it becomes supersaturated. At this point, there is more sugar in the solution than can remain dissolved at the cooler temperature, and some of the sugar starts to come out of the solution and join the sugar crystals on the string. After a few days, your crystals should be quite large — big enough to eat! What you've done in this experiment is to reverse a process. You've taken a solution and caused the molecules to turn back into crystals.

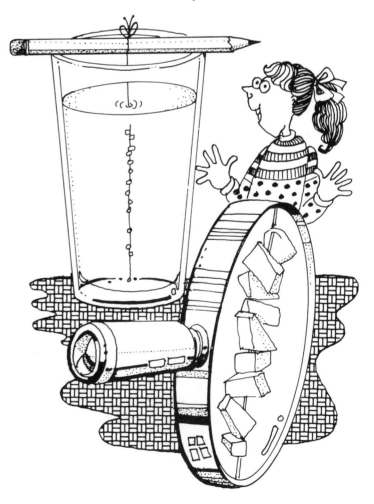

INSIDE STORY OF POP

WHAT's the formula for soda pop? It could be F + F = P (Fizz plus Flavour equals Pop).

Pop began as fizzy water that people added flavouring to. Why did they want fizzy water to start with? Because they thought it was healthy, just as they believed the bubbly waters of natural springs had powers to cure them of all sorts of ills.

Although the first artificial bubbly water was made in 1722, it wasn't until 1832 that carbonated beverages became really popular. That's when John Matthews invented a machine to inject carbonated gas into water.

People then started experimenting with adding flavour to the bubbly water to give it more taste. They also added the bubbly water to some of the beverages and potions they already had, to make them taste better. Within a short time, the familiar pops of today were developed—from colas to ginger ales. Of course, not all tastes were popular. For some reason, spinach and eggplant soda pop never caught on.

Make your own ginger ale

You'll need:
180 mL (¾ c) peeled, grated ginger root
a large glass jar with lid
1 L (4 c) cold water
another large jar or bowl
a wire strainer
a coffee filter (nylon or paper)
sugar

1. Place the grated ginger in the glass jar. Add the cold water and put the lid on the jar. Let it sit for 24 hours.
2. Pour the liquid through the wire strainer into a bowl. Rinse out the jar you steeped the ginger in and throw away the ginger.
3. Pour the liquid through the coffee filter back into the clean jar.
4. Add sugar a little at a time until it's sweet enough for you. Try it plain or mixed with soda water. Do a "taste test" with your family and friends. Which way do most people prefer it?

HERE'S a scientific centrepiece that's so unusual it's bound to be a conversation piece too.

You'll need:
a tall glass jar or pitcher
some white vinegar
baking soda
vegetable dye
mothballs (available at most hardware stores)

1. Fill the pitcher with water, then very slowly stir in about three spoonfuls of vinegar and two spoonfuls of baking soda. The liquid will start to fizz. (You might have to adjust the amount of vinegar and baking soda to the size of your pitcher. Just be sure there's always three parts vinegar to every two of baking soda.)
2. Add a couple of drops of vegetable dye — not too much — and drop in a few mothballs. The mothballs will sink to the bottom at first, but then they'll start to rise. When they reach the top of the liquid, they sink again and they'll keep doing this at least long enough for you to have dinner.

How does it work?
Your unusual centrepiece is caused by a chemical reaction. The vinegar is an acid and the baking soda is a base. When you combine them, you cause a chemical reaction that produces carbon dioxide bubbles.

Bubbles tend to gather on surfaces, as you may have noticed when you've put a straw into a soft drink. They gather in great numbers on the mothballs. Since a mothball isn't very heavy, the bubbles clinging to it soon lift it to the surface. When it reaches the top, the bubbles break, the mothball sinks back to the bottom, and starts collecting bubbles again.

The vegetable dye: that's just to make it pretty! You could make several containers of mothballs and dye them different colours for a larger centrepiece.

By the way, you can get the same effect by dropping salted peanuts into a soft drink!

INVISIBLE INK

ERE'S a way to write secret messages —
messages so secret, they're invisible.

You'll need:
vinegar or lemon juice for ink
a toothpick or paintbrush to write with
a piece of paper
a candle in a holder

1. Dip a toothpick or paintbrush into your invisible
   ink and write your message on a piece of paper.
   When the message is dry, the paper will look blank.
2. To read the secret message, pass the paper back and
   forth over the flame of the candle. Ask your parents
   to help with this and be sure you don't let the paper
   catch fire. Gradually the writing will appear.

How does it work?
That heat from the flame causes a chemical change in
the dried ink. The portion of the paper which
absorbed the vinegar or lemon juice chars at a lower
temperature than the untreated paper, so the writing
shows up as a faint brown scorching.

Secret Writing Tips
1. If you're using a toothpick for a pen, write with
   the round end. That way you won't scratch or
   tear the paper.
2. Don't press too hard when you're writing your
   message. If you do, you'll make an impression
   on the paper that can be read even without
   decoding it over a flame.

ERE are three unusual bubble experiments. Before you get started on them, mix up a batch of superbubbles.

Superbubbles
Mix together and gently shake the following:
6 glasses of water
2 glasses *clear* dishwashing liquid detergent (Joy® is the best)
1 - 4 glasses glycerine—4 is best, but because of the cost of glycerine, you may wish to use less than 4 glasses (You can buy this at any drugstore.)

Monster Bubbles
These bubbles are so big they look as if a monster made them.

You'll need:
a thin wire coat hanger
superbubble mixture

1. Undo the coat hanger and twist it into a big circle.
2. Dip it into the superbubble goop and blow. With a little practice, you'll soon be blowing huge bubbles.

How does it work?
When you add soap to the water, you loosen the hold that the water molecules have on each other. This makes the water more "stretchable" so you can blow bigger bubbles. The glycerine makes the bubbles last longer than usual.

Slow Breakers
Most bubbles pop instantly when you puncture them, but not these.

You'll need:
superbubble mixture
a funnel
a piece of string about 20 cm (9 inches) long
a sharp pencil

1. Tie a piece of string around the stem of the funnel so that the string hangs down below the funnel.
2. Tie a loop in the loose end of the string.
3. Dip the big end of the funnel, string and all, into the superbubble goop.
4. Remove it and blow a big bubble by blowing into the stem of the funnel. The string will lie along the outer surface of the bubble.

5. Using a sharp pencil, poke a hole in the bubble through the loop of the string and watch what happens. First, the loop of string will stretch into a perfect circle. Then the bubble will slowly collapse.

How does it work?

Why doesn't the bubble pop instantly when you puncture it? The string prevents a long tear from developing in the soap film. The bubble can collapse only as quickly as air can escape through the small hole inside the string.

Soap Film

Soap film is a bubble with no air in it. As you'll see by trying a couple of experiments, soap film is pretty interesting too.

You'll need:
superbubble mixture
a thin wire coat hanger

1. Undo the coat hanger and bend it into a rectangular shape.
2. Dip this frame into the superbubble goop (you

might have to pour the bubble mixture into a flat pan so that you can dip the whole frame in at once). Hold the framed soap film up to the light. You'll see a rainbow of colours. This is caused by light reflecting from the front and back surfaces of the film.
3. Now, dry the frame and tie string to it in the pattern shown. Don't stretch it tight; let it hang limply.
4. Dip the frame, string and all, into the superbubble goop. Lift it out and prick a hole in the centre loop. What happens to the shape of the centre loop?

How does it work?

Why does the string form a perfect circle? Soap film always shrinks to its smallest possible area. For the soap film to be as small as possible in area, the loop of string has to be as large as possible in area. A circle is the shape that lets the loop of string cover the most area.

Now that you've solved that mystery, try making a hole in a different part of the frame. Can you see the outline of part of a circle? Try bursting the sections one part at a time and see what happens to the string.

159

YOU can be a draft detective. Most buildings leak air through tiny holes and cracks that are hard to find. Track down those cold rivers of air that chill your back when you lie on the floor. You can do it! All you need is a draftometer.

You'll need:
scissors
a strip of tissue paper or tissue
tape
a long pencil

1. Tape one end of the paper or tissue along the length of the pencil.
2. Blow gently on the tissue to make sure it's well taped. See how easily it responds to air movement!
3. Hold the draftometer near the edges of the windows and doors in your house. (If your home is heated by a forced air furnace, wait until the fan is off before you use your draftometer.)
4. If your home has a fireplace, hold the draftometer in front of it and test what happens with the damper open and closed.

   Once you've found all the air leaks, it's a simple job for the family handyperson to plug them up.

What makes a draft?
Air leaks through the cracks in your house. In the winter, this lets cold air in from the outside and allows the hot air to escape. Therefore, the inside temperature cools down and energy is wasted. In the summer, the same leaks let the cool, house air out and allow summer's heat to pour in.

Cold air is denser than warm air; therefore it tends to fall — that's why you usually feel cold drafts along the floor. Warm air moves in to take the place of falling cold air. So when you open your refrigerator door, you not only lose the nice cold air that is inside, but warm air flows in and the refrigerator has to work even harder to cool it off.

Check this out
Open the refrigerator door a crack and hold your draftometer at the bottom, in front of the opening. Close the door and try it again, this time holding your draftometer at the top. Which way does it blow?

How do movies move? Here's how to make a toy, called a thaumatrope, that will reveal the secret.

You'll need:
a pen and paper
glue
some stiff cardboard
scissors
string

1. Trace the circles illustrated and their drawings onto a piece of paper. Be sure to mark in the dots (•) and stars (*).
2. Cut out the two paper circles and one cardboard circle the same size.
3. Glue the paper circles on opposite sides of the cardboard disk. Make sure that the stars are opposite each other.
4. Carefully punch tiny holes where the dots appear and thread string through them, as shown.
5. Twirl the disk by first twirling the string. As you twirl, watch the bird and cage. Like magic, the bird will appear to be inside the cage.

How does it work?

Your eye holds onto the image of the bird for a split second after it's gone. By that time the cage is in sight, and you seem to see the bird in the cage. The same thing happens at the movies. If you look at a piece of movie film, you'll see that it is a series of pictures separated by black spaces.

When a picture is flashed on the screen, your eye retains the image for a fraction of a second afterwards, so you don't see the moments of darkness between the frames. This is called persistence of vision. When a series of still pictures of moving objects is flashed before your eyes very quickly, you see them as uninterrupted movement. In order for this to work, at least 16 images must be flashed on the screen every second.

When you go to the movies, you see 24 images flashed on the screen every second, separated by intervals of darkness of the same length. So, in fact, you spend about half of a movie in the dark!

MAGNETIC IMAGES

YOU'VE probably drawn with crayons, paints, and coloured pencils, but have you ever painted patterns with pieces of metal? Here's a fun and easy way to create a picture to hang on your wall.

You'll need:
two magnets
fine steel wool
stiff paper or light cardboard (file cards are ideal)
old scissors
hair spray or clear, plastic fixative spray
some metal objects such as paper clips, nails, etc.

1. Cut the steel wool into tiny pieces with the scissors.
2. Put the magnet on a table and place the sheet of paper over it.
3. Generously sprinkle some steel wool filings on the paper. You'll see that the filings have collected into a pattern.
4. Tap the paper gently to change the pattern or move the paper over the magnet until you're satisfied with the pattern.
5. If you have two magnets, put them both under a piece of paper and watch what happens to the filing patterns when you move the magnets around. Try putting the magnets end to end, top to end, and top to top to see what you can create.
6. If you have any other metal objects handy, put them under the paper to see what patterns they cause in the filings. Touch these objects to the magnets to see if you can magnetize them to help make your picture even more dramatic.
7. When you finish your metal paintings, clean up any scattered or fallen filings by covering your magnet with a piece of paper, then passing it closely over your work area.
8. When you have a pattern of filings that you want to keep, spray it several times with hair spray, or clear, plastic fixative, while the magnet is still in place. Let it dry between sprayings.

How does it work?

When you sprinkled the filings onto the paper on top of the magnet, you probably noticed that they formed a pattern. And when you tapped the paper gently, the filings collected even more definitely along the pattern lines.

These lines indicate the field of force that reaches out from the magnet. When the paper is moved over the magnet, the filings shift to follow the force field.

If you've played with magnets before, you may have already discovered that they have two poles, usually called north and south. If you put the north pole of one magnet near the south pole of another, they pull towards, or attract, each other. But if you put the two north poles or the two south poles together, they push one another away. You can see the difference in your magnet drawings.

When you touched the other metal objects to the magnet, you may have discovered that some of them became magnets themselves, as long as they remained in contact wth your original magnets. Some even stayed magnetized after they were separated from the original magnet. You can test this by putting the separate metal objects under a paper covered with metal filings.

AVE you ever watched a house being built? Under the bricks or siding, there's a frame of wooden beams — the skeleton of the house. The frame gives the building its strength. It's not difficult to build a frame that would hold up a house. Test your construction skills by building with beams made of newspaper.

You'll need:
sheets of old newspaper (make sure everyone has read them!)
toothpicks
tape

1. Lay a sheet of newspaper flat on the floor. Place a toothpick across one corner and roll the newspaper tightly around the toothpick until the whole sheet is rolled. Fasten it with the tape. If you've rolled tightly enough, you'll have a long, strong, newspaper dowel that is very hard to bend. (If you want to shorten it, cut off the ends.)

2. Repeat the above process until you have a pile of newspaper beams.

3. When you're ready to start building, attach the beams together with tape. Start by outlining the shape of your building on the floor, using the beams. Then build up.

4. As you build, you might have to brace your frame with crossbeams.

5. Build your building as high as you can. Can you make it reach the ceiling?

SUPER STRUCTURES

THE next time you see a house or a high-rise under construction, look at the shapes made by the frame. Some shapes are stronger than others. You don't need steel girders to experiment with shapes. You can raid the kitchen for building materials.

You'll need:
a package of toothpicks
miniature marshmallows (or modelling clay)
a hardcover book
2 chairs
5 quarters in a paper cup

1. Using the toothpicks as beams and the marshmallows (or balls of modelling clay) as glue, try to build a tall structure using nine marshmallows and 15 toothpicks.
2. Now try building with 15 marshmallows and nine toothpicks. Which structure is stronger? When you look at the stronger one, do you see more triangles?
3. Using 14 marshmallows and 20 toothpicks, try to make a structure that's strong enough to hold the book.
4. Here's a final challenge: Try building a bridge between two chairs 30 cm (1 foot) apart. Use as many marshmallows and toothpicks as necessary. When you're done, see if it will hold the cup full of quarters.

Note: If you want to make bigger, stronger and more permanent structures, attach the toothpicks with glue instead of marshmallows.

THE SCIENCE OF FUN

LOOK down on any baseball field just before a game and you might see a few players who look as though they're playing the game under water. They're slowly lobbing the ball back and forth or gently swinging the bat at imaginary balls.

These players are doing a slow-motion version of hitting and catching to start the blood flowing more quickly to the right muscles. This supplies the muscles with extra oxygen and raises their temperature. Warm muscles are stronger and have more endurance. A warmed-up baseball pitcher puts greater speed and distance into his throws, while warmed-up sprinters and marathoners get better running times.

Stretching exercises are another popular type of warm-up routine. Toe touches, hip rotations and other stretching activities loosen up the elastic parts of the body—the muscles, tendons and ligaments—and lower the risk of sports injuries. Football players, for example, are often fanatical about stretching, and more than a few wide receivers can rival any ballerina in doing the splits.

And by the way, human athletes aren't the only ones who warm up. If you've ever seen a horse race, you might have noticed the jockeys leading their horses slowly around the track or taking them for a gallop just prior to starting time. Horses are like people—they're better off warm than colt.

The best exercises for any particular sport are those that use the motions of that sport. But there are many general warm-up exercises that are great for any sport. Here are some you can do any time you're planning to run, skate, throw, hop, skip or jump.

Hold yourself in each position while you count 15 seconds. Feel your muscles stretch, but not so much that it hurts.

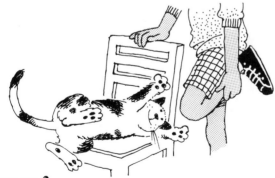

Warm up 1
Bend forward and stretch down until you touch your toes. You can bend your knees a little, if that helps you reach your toes, then straighten them slowly once you get down there. Don't bounce!

Warm up 2
Steady yourself with one hand on a wall or chair back. Grab the back of your ankle with the other hand and bend your leg up until your heel touches your bum. Hold.

Warm up 3
Bending sideways at your waist, run hand as far down your leg as you can and hold.

Warm up 4
This is a good exercise to do before you run. Shift your weight to one foot, then raise the other foot so it's resting on the ball of the foot and rotate your ankle in one direction, then the other. Do the same with the other foot.

Weird warm up
Here's the warm up: squat like a frog, put your elbows inside your knees and push out. What's the sport? If you guessed basketball, congratulations. This warm up stretches the muscles you need for the sideways shifting that basketball players do.

READ the title of this page out loud.
That's about how long it takes for a big league fastball to move from the pitcher's hand to home plate—41/100 of a second. That's fast!

Many coaches and trainers say that if you want to be a top athlete, you've got to have a fast reaction time. You've got to be able to start to swing a bat or stop a puck or dive for the spiked ball in the blink of an eye.

How fast is your reaction time?

You'll need:
a friend
a ruler

1. Hold one end of the ruler so that the other end is between your friend's thumb and middle finger, as shown in the picture. The "1 inch" mark should be right between her fingers.
2. Without warning, drop the ruler. Your friend must catch it between her two fingers.
3. Note the spot where your friend caught the ruler. Now you try it.

The lower the number at the point where you catch the ruler, the faster your reaction time, the time it takes for you to start moving.

Were you the fastest? The slowest? No matter how you ranked among your friends, as far as most sport goes, *it doesn't mean a thing*.

To understand why reaction speed alone isn't important, try the test again. This time, do it by yourself. Hold the ruler with one hand and try to catch it with the other. How did your reaction time improve so much in such a short time?

The answer is, it didn't. You probably still started to move at the same speed as before. But

this time you knew when the ruler was going to drop. Your ability to anticipate was more important than your ability to start moving quickly.

Similarly, most good athletes don't need to be superfast at reacting. Sprinters are an exception; they must react quickly to the start signal. In most cases it's what an athlete can predict about the course of the event that really counts. The champion boxer Muhammed Ali, famous for his speed and timing in a sport where both count a lot, had only an average reaction time. But he was way above average in his understanding of the sport and what his opponents were likely to do.

If you're a shortstop in baseball, for example, there's just no way you can merely react quickly enough to catch every ball that heads your way. Instead, you have to anticipate where the batter is going to hit the ball. When the ball does indeed head that way, and you're there to catch it, you look like a genius with lightning reflexes.

Squash is the same. It looks like a game that demands fast reaction time. But beginners and experienced players may have exactly the same reaction times. The difference is that beginning squash players have no idea where the ball is going to bounce so they scurry all over trying to keep up with it. But from hours and hours of time on the court, the experienced player knows exactly where the bouncing ball is going to be.

The better you are at predicting what will happen next in a sport, the less fast you have to be. If you're ready and waiting for the ball, or the puck or the punch, reaction time is of little importance.

WANT to give your brain a workout?
Try this.

You'll need:
two pieces of paper
a pen
a stopwatch or a watch with a second hand

1. Make a list of 20 three-letter words such as toy, ark, box, she, etc.
2. Make a second list using the same words but with the letters all mixed up so that toy becomes yot, ark becomes kra, box becomes xob and she becomes seh, and so on.
3. Ask a friend to read out loud the first list and time him.
4. Ask him to read out loud the second list and time him again. Which time was faster?

Why?
You respond more quickly to familiar patterns.

What's the point?
Well, it could have a lot to do with being an expert hockey player like Wayne Gretzky. Or a chess grand master. Or a great shortstop. They all learn to recognize the patterns in their games.

To become an expert hockey player, you have to do two things. Number one, you have to sharpen your physical skills—skating, handling the puck, checking. Number two, you have to understand that learning to play hockey is just like learning how to read.

Remember the day you picked up your first book? You opened it, and there, staring back at you, was a jumble of squiggles that made no sense. But with practice, you soon discovered that the squiggles formed letters and the letters gathered together to form words. The nonsense turned into sense.

The same thing happens when you watch your

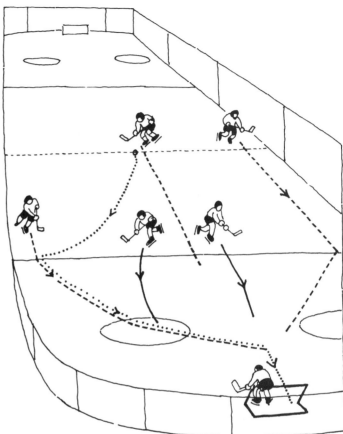

first hockey game. All you can see is a bunch of players scattered across the ice, like jumbled-up letters on a page. But the more you watch, the more clearly you pick out how those players are working together as a team. From one set of positions, the players move to another, to another, and another, just like letters rearranging themselves to form different words.

A hockey team can arrange itself into hundreds of patterns during the course of one game. Just as it takes a long time to build up a good vocabulary of words, it also takes a long time to recognize all the patterns in hockey. But once you've learned the patterns, you always know what to do in every situation—when to pass the puck, when to check an opponent, and so on. Even better, you start to anticipate what will happen next. They say that Gretzky knows where the puck will be three seconds before it gets there.

Scientists estimate that it takes 10 000 hours of practice to recognize all the patterns that players can fall into on the ice. Practice really does make perfect. Expert hockey players are made, not born.

Soccer, basketball, football, chess—each of these is like hockey; the players must learn to recognize the patterns of the game. But there are other sports where patterns are less important.

In volleyball, for example, you will acquire the ability to scan and find the position of the ball. Expert volleyball players don't watch the other players so much as they focus on the speeding ball, which can be flying through the air at speeds of up to 145 km/h (90 mph). Once again, this ability to scan takes thousands of hours of practice.

Whether the game is hockey or volleyball or soccer, it all goes to show you that every sport asks you to use your brain as well as your body.

 HAT kind of game could you play with your eyes closed? How about this one?

You'll need:
a foam ball
some jingle bells
needle and thread or a safety pin or tape or glue
one or more friends
kerchiefs or strips of cloth to use as blindfolds

1. Sew or pin or tape or glue the bells to the foam ball.
2. Close your eyes and tell your friends to close theirs, or put on blindfolds.
3. Roll the ball to a friend and have it rolled back. You need to listen carefully to the bells.
4. If there are several of you, try rolling it back and forth across a circle.

If you find it a challenge to locate and catch a ball with just your ears to guide you, imagine playing a team sport with your eyes closed.

Actually, there is such a sport. It's called goal ball and it's played mainly by people with little or no vision. Like you, they wear blindfolds to give everyone the same chance. There are three players on a side and the teams take turns trying to get a jingling basketball-sized ball into one another's goal. Players use all parts of their body to defend the goal, even making spectacular diving saves when necessary.

As you've discovered, it requires concentration and quiet to listen for the jingling, so goal ball audiences are silent, cheering only when there's a halt in the play.

If you think playing ball's difficult when you can't see, how about running a race? You not only have to concentrate on moving fast but you have to do it without banging into anything. One solution is to run holding on to a tether held by a sighted person for guidance. But when you're holding a rope, you can't use both arms for running. And arms are important for balance. Besides, the sighted person then leads.

The other solution is to run in front of a sighted person who guides you with taps on your hip or inside your elbow. That way your body is free to run and you can go at your own pace.

One sport in which a blind athlete must run without physical guidance is the long jump. The only difference in the sport for those who can't see is that the take-off area is a metre (yard) long instead of being marked by a board. It's covered with talcum powder and the jump is measured from the athlete's last footprint in the powder. The athlete starts at the take-off area, then walks back to the start, counting off the paces. The athlete must run alone down the runway and take off without outside cues. Some blind runners use callers, people who stand at the far end of the pit and yell out a repeated sound which the jumper can use for orientation, but they are not allowed to tell the athlete when to jump.

Take a guided tour

You'll need:
a friend
a blindfold
some small pieces of paper
a clear, grassy area

1. Lay out a course to follow by dropping pieces of paper on the ground. (Be sure to pick them up when you're through.)
2. Put on the blindfold.
3. Walk the course, with your friend behind you, tapping you on your hip or elbow to guide you. How fast can you walk?

Running blind

How hard is it to run in a straight line without looking and without guidance?

You'll need:
a long-jump pit (look for one on the athletic field at your local high school)
two friends
a blindfold

1. Position a friend on either side of the runway to tell you when to stop or catch you if you go off course.
2. Stand at the starting line and put on the blindfold.
3. Run to the take-off point.

How quickly do you go off course? In which direction? Which hand do you usually use? You'll tend to veer in that direction.

o you think sports are a drag? If so, you're right.

Drag is the resistance you feel when you skate, ski, bicycle or run fast. You encounter drag as you move through the air (or water). Drag opposes motion.

Skiing Eggs

Downhill skiers aren't being chicken when they crouch with their chests to their knees as they ski. They're doing the "egg." This skiing position was developed after putting skiers in a wind tunnel and having them scramble from one position to another while scientists measured air resistance.

These hard-boiled tests revealed that the "egg" is the best shape for downhill racing. They also found that protruding buckles on a skier's boots can add 0.3 seconds to every minute of a racer's time because they increase drag! That 0.3 is a mighty big number when skiing victories are measured in hundredths of a second.

Bent Skaters

Speed skaters have found that bending over with only their head and shoulders facing into the wind cuts down the amount of surface area hitting the air and is the best way to reduce drag. (The arm that swings back and forth does so to maintain the skater's balance.)

Drag-Free Clothes

Most sports clothing is definitely not a drag. The smoother the material, the less drag there is. Think of the shiny, form-fitting suits the speed skaters wear. The same applies to water sports, too. Competitive swimmers even shave their bodies to make their skin smoother and freer from drag.

On the other hand, you can go too far in combatting drag. Not long ago, one ski wear designer made a plastic fabric so smooth that skiers who fell couldn't stop themselves from sliding down the mountain. The plastic skin was so slippery that there wasn't enough friction between the plastic and the snow to slow down the skier's slide.

Drag is an obstacle in many sports, and the faster the sport, the greater the drag. If you increase your speed by ten times, your drag could increase by one hundred times! You can probably think of lots of sports where overcoming drag is important. What about horse racing, where jockeys curl over the horse in their own version of the egg? And how about drag racing?

But can you think of a sport in which competitors look at drag as a blessing? You're right if you guessed skydiving. If you were skydiving, you'd want to slow down the rate at which you moved through the air. Without a parachute on your back to pop open and give you some much-needed drag, your meeting with the ground would be a real drag.

If you have a bicycle, you can experience the effects of drag.

You'll need:
a bicycle
a hill away from traffic
a stopwatch or a watch with a second hand

1. With just a push off, coast down the hill, sitting straight up as if you were driving a car. Clock yourself and note the time.
2. Do it again, but this time crouch down into the egg position. Clock yourself again and compare the results. Was there a difference? Why?

If you don't have a bicycle

You'll need:
a spoon
a tub full of water
sifted flour

1. Sprinkle the sifted flour on top of the water until it forms a thin, uniform layer.
2. Run the bowl of the spoon through the surface of the water. Feel the resistance in the handle of the spoon? That's drag. The turbulence patterns you see in the water are caused by the energy used in overcoming drag.

I MAGINE what it would be like to pedal your bike ten times faster than normal—as fast as a dragster. A *bicycle* really did go that fast a couple of years ago on the Bonneville Speedway in northwestern Utah.

To start out, the bicycle and its rider were towed behind a high-powered car. Attached to the rear of the car was a large rectangular windscreen, which formed a wall between the car and the bike. When the car reached about 100 km/h (60 mph), the tow chain was cut, setting the cyclist free to pedal on his own. Instead of losing speed, the cyclist kept on accelerating right along with the car, eventually reaching an incredible 226 km/h (140.5 mph).

How could the cyclist go so fast? By taking advantage of the windblocking effect of the car ahead, which cyclists call its *draft*. Behind the large windscreen, it was as if the bicycle were moving through a hole in the air.

You'll need:
a cardboard toilet-paper roll
a long aluminum foil pan or cookie sheet
matches and permission to use them
two household candles
tape

Creating a draft

1. Light the candles and use some of their melted wax to stick them to the foil pan or cookie sheet about 10 cm (5 inches) apart. Place the toilet-paper roll upright on the pan about 2 cm (an inch) in front of one of the candles and stick it in place with tape.
2. Pull the pan past you with the toilet roll leading. Keep your eyes on the two flames. In what direction are the candle flames blowing?

As the toilet roll moves through the air, it pushes the air aside, creating an area of lower air pressure just behind it. Air from outside that area rushes in to the low-pressure spot, pushing the flame nearest the toilet rolls forward. The flame is drafting.

Imagine that the toilet roll is the leading cyclist in a race and you'll get an idea of why racing cyclists line up one behind the other during a race. They, too, are "drafting."

On level ground overcoming wind resistance consumes about 80 per cent of a bicycle racer's energy. When a racer pulls up close behind another bicycle and drafts, it takes much less energy to push away the air in front of her.

While riding in a draft saves energy, creating the draft uses a lot of energy. That's why the members of cycling teams take turns being the leader.

Cutting through the wind
You'll need:
the same equipment as before, plus
a piece of paper

1. Cut a piece of paper into a rectangle the same height as the toilet roll and long enough to wrap around it and extend about 2 cm (an inch) past on either side. Bend it into a tear-drop shape and tape the ends together. Drop it over the toilet-paper roll with the sharp end pointing toward the candle.

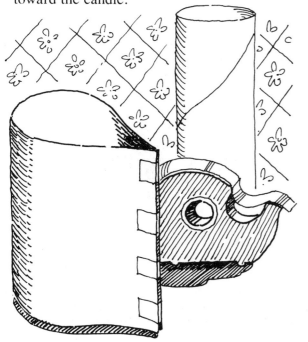

2. Pull the pan past you again. Keep your eyes on the flames. Do they behave any differently this time?

The tear drop shape of the paper allows the air to flow around the toilet roll with less resistance, making it easier for the tube to move through the air. This eliminates the draft behind it. If you were riding behind the leader in a bike race, would you rather follow someone shaped like a toilet roll or a streamlined tear drop?

Stay Out of the Draft
The technique of "drafting" is not something to try on your own. It's difficult to learn and requires proper coaching because it can be dangerous. Such close following often is the reason for those disastrous pile-ups in bike races.

Drafting isn't the only way to decrease wind resistance on a bike. You can also enclose the wheel spokes, as is done on the best racing bicycles. Enclosed spokes (or solid wheels) create less air turbulence, making the bicycle more aerodynamic.

You could also take the whole subject of air resistance lying down. Especially if you're behind the wheel of a "recumbent" bicycle, which resembles a streamlined space pod, since it's enclosed in a shell made of lightweight plastic or fibreglass. You ride these bikes in a reclining position, as if you were steering a sled or toboggan.

WOULD you like to lose some weight in a real hurry?

You'll need:
a set of bathroom scales

1. Stand up straight on the bathroom scales and take note of how much you weigh.
2. Lower yourself quickly by bending at the knees. What happens to the reading of your weight?

What you just did on the bathroom scales was **unweight** yourself. Unweighting is a technique that downhill skiers use to do turns. Unweighting requires you to bend your knees just before entering the turn. This lifts your body's weight off the skis for a brief moment, making it easier to turn the skis in a new direction.

Why do you lose weight so suddenly? When you bend your knees suddenly, you remove the support from under your upper body, which leaves it falling through space and only your feet pressing down on the skis (or bathroom scale). If you are quick enough, even the weight of your feet will be absent.

Unweighting lasts for only the split second that your body is falling through the air. When you stop bending your knees, the force of your body hitting the skis is so great that you suddenly "gain" a lot of extra weight—you blimp out for a moment.

Even if you've never skied, unweighting is probably familiar to you, though you may not have recognized it as such. Remember the last time you were walking barefooted and stepped on a sharp object? What was your immediate response? You probably bent your knee, dropped your hips and rushed your other foot forward to support your weight. In doing this, you reduced the force holding your foot against the sharp object—you unweighted your foot.

TURN, TURN, TURN

WHICH of these figure skaters do you think would twirl the fastest?

If just thinking about it makes you dizzy, try tracing the figures onto cardboard and cutting them out. Then stick a pin where the dot is and try spinning them. Give them each the same amount of "push". Do you notice a difference? Is one harder to spin than the other? It may be hard to tell on the models, but in real life, the sit-spinning skater would twirl much faster and more easily than the one with her arms stretched out.

What would happen if a skater changed positions while spinning? If you have a stool or chair that spins, you can find out.

1. Sit on the stool or chair with your arms outstretched.
2. Spin yourself or, even better, get someone else to spin you.
3. As you're spinning, fold your arms in tightly against your body.

Why do you and the figure skaters spin more slowly when you're stretched out than when you're tucked in?

A spinning object has angular momentum, a special property which is a product of the object's mass, radius (how far it extends from the centre of rotation) and rate of spin.

One of the things that makes angular momentum so special is that it always stays the same. This means that if you increase your radius while spinning (by stretching your arms out), either your rate of spin or your mass must decrease to keep the angular momentum the same. Since you're not likely to lose any mass (unless you go on a crash diet while spinning!) your rate of spin slows down instead. If you make your radius smaller by bringing your arms in, your rate of spin speeds up again.

WHICH is faster, arms or legs? That may sound like a funny question. After all, who races with their arms?

Wheelchair athletes do.

But can wheelchair racers push as fast as legged athletes can stride? You bet! In a marathon race between a top runner and a top wheelchair athlete, the competitor in the wheelchair would not only win, he'd have time for a shower and a cold drink before his opponent reached the finish line.

Giving 'Em the Gears

Everyone is familiar with the gears on a bike, but not many people realize that a wheelchair has "gears," too.

On a bike, changing gears means flipping a lever so that your bike chain changes to a different size of ring. On a wheelchair, you change gears by moving your hands between the outer and inner rims. Both produce the same result. Gripping the smaller, inner rim gives you more power per push: the wheel travels farther for the distance your hand has to move, but it takes more effort for you to move it. If you push the small rim while you're moving, you get more speed, but it's very hard to get started from a standstill this way. On the other hand, gripping the large outer rim makes it easier to move the wheel, but your hand has to travel a lot farther compared to how far the wheel goes. So the outer rim is your better "starting gear."

Shooting from the Hip

When a standing athlete tosses a basketball into the basket, she uses her whole body to propel it. A wheelchair athlete may have muscle control only in her arms and shoulders. This adds to the skill required to get the basketball into the basket as you can see for yourself.

You'll need:
a kitchen chair
a basketball
a hoop (or pick a point on an outside wall that's about hoop height)

1. Position the chair so it faces your hoop.
2. Keeping your body in contact with the chair, try to throw the basketball into the hoop.

Do you use different muscles than you would when throwing from a standing position?

THE WIDE WORLD OF SPORTS

WHAT's your favourite sport? Tossing the caber? Octopush? Sepak takraw? Never heard of any of them? You don't know what you're missing.

Tossing the Caber

Hoot maun, whit's yer caber? In the Heelands of Scotland yer caber looks a wee bit like a telephone pole, except that it's nae attached to the grun. It's a smooth, tapered tree trunk that guid kilted laddies toss durin' their annual Heeland Games.

The lad maks a platform wi' his hands and hulds the narrow end, leanin' the heavy pole agin' his shoulder. He then takes a run and heaves the pole into the air, aimin' for the perfect toss, wi' the caber landin' on its heid, then floppin' owr and smackin' the grun wi' its base pintin' awa from the competitor. It's nae how far the lad tosses that counts, it's the accuracy.

Octopush

Contrary to what you might expect, octopush is not a pushing match with an octopus. Introduced in South Africa in the 1960s, octopush is hockey played underwater. Players don skin-diving equipment, jump into a swimming pool, and with miniature hockey sticks and an ice-hockey puck, play by the normal rules of hockey on the pool bottom.

Of course, real hockey is always played on ice. Which is why the Canadian version of octopush dips below the surface of frozen ponds and lakes. Players outfitted in scuba gear enter the frigid water through a hole in the ice. Standing upside down with their fins against the ice, they play hockey with sticks and an inflated beach ball.

Canadian octopush is still largely an oddity, enjoyed by only a few. But who knows, every popular sport was once unusual and had only a few enthusiasts!

Sepak Takraw

Americans are crazy about baseball, Canadians hockey, Argentinians soccer, and Malaysians sepak takraw.

Sepak takraw is like volleyball, and it isn't. It's like volleyball in that two teams compete against each other across a net, and the ball must not hit the ground. It's unlike volleyball in that the ball is smaller and the top of the net is only about shoulder height. A takraw ball is made of woven rattan, has a hollow middle and is about the size of a softball.

But the real difference between volleyball and sepak takraw—and the real challenge to the sport—is that you can't hit the ball with your hands. Feet, knees, head, shoulders, elbows are okay, but no hands! It's said that keeping the takraw ball in the air calls for the speed of badminton, the dexterity of football and the teamwork of volleyball.

Sepak takraw has many rules but you might want to try a less complicated version of the game, called in-tossing takraw, which is played usually as a training exercise.

In-Tossing Takraw

You'll Need:

a takraw ball, but if you can't find one, improvise.
A takraw ball is 40 cm (16 inches) in circumference and weighs 200 g (7 ounces). A ball of crumpled paper works well. Or try a hollow ball made of plastic, or a foam rubber ball with similar dimensions.
a group of players

The object of in-tossing takraw is to see how many times, and in how many different ways, a group of players can keep the takraw ball in the air without it touching the ground.

The game is most fun when you try more difficult or stylish shots. A simple kick is easiest, while shots with knees, elbows, heads or shoulders are harder. Try the classic takraw shot, which involves kicking the ball with both feet together behind the back. Remember: hands are not allowed in takraw!

One legendary takraw player, named Daeng, was said to have an infinite number of shots. His most spectacular feat, though, was dropping down on all fours and then rebounding from the ground, striking the ball with his rump on the way up. Can you do a "Daeng" shot?

GOOD evening, people in radioland, and welcome again to *The Sport of Munching*. I'm Doctor Professor Frank Furter, and each week at this time I answer your questions about food and health. Tonight my topic is "Sports and Good Nutrition," and already I can see that my telephone hot line is heating up. So let's see who my first caller is. Hello, you're on the air.

Hi, Dr. Frank. My name's Charlene and I'd like to know if I can get extra energy by eating a candy bar just before I run in a track meet.

Charlene, think of your body as a car engine. It must be fueled regularly or else it will run down. The "gasoline" that you put into your "tank" comes mostly from food that is high in carbohydrates (the starches or sugars found in bread, fruits and vegetables, noodles, rice and potatoes).

Inside your digestive system, carbohydrates are broken down into glucose, which is a simple sugar that is shipped to your muscles to fuel their contractions.

Try this, Charlene. Pop an unsalted cracker into your mouth and chew on it for about a minute. Do you notice any change in the flavour? The mushy cracker should taste a little sweeter because the saliva in your mouth has begun to break down the carbohydrates in the cracker into sugar.

Chocolate is loaded with sugar, so you might think that a pre-game candy bar will give you a burst of energy. However, the exact opposite is true. High doses of sugar stimulate your body to remove glucose from the blood. So, by eating a chocolate bar or any other sweet treat before a game, you're stealing glucose away from your muscles at the very moment when they need it most.

Next caller please.

Hi, Dr. Frank, this is Bubba calling. The guys down at the health spa say that I have to pig out on protein if I want to build big muscles. Are they right?

Well, I could say it's all hog-wash but it is true that protein is the building block of muscle tissue. However, the amount of protein you need for building and repairing muscle tissue is not all that large, even if you're working out several times a week.

Unfortunately, many athletes think that they can have big muscles by gorging on protein. And so they eat lots of protein-rich foods—meat, milk and fish—and may even go so far as to consume expensive protein drinks and supplements.

The truth is, Bubba, that a well-balanced diet provides you with all the protein you need.

Next question.

Dr. Frank, my name is Julio and I play centre on my high school basketball team. My problem is that my mother always cooks me a couple of hamburgers and a plate of fries right before I leave for a game. Is it okay to play with so much food in my stomach?

Sure, Julio. After all, in basketball you're always trying to throw up, if you'll excuse the pun. Seriously, many athletes do put away a feast of meat and potatoes just before game time. But they'd be better off without it. A full stomach interferes with breathing. As well, the stomach muscles need extra blood to help them do the work of digesting; this diverts blood away from the muscles you use to play basketball.

Hamburgers and steaks, in particular, make a bad pre-game meal. Because they're high in protein and fat, they take a long time to digest. Tell your mother that you must avoid food for one hour before a game.

Next caller, please.

Dr. Frank, I'm Totie and I'm training to be a competitive figure skater, so I'd like to stay as slim as I can. What I want to know is, should I cut out fatty foods?

You'd be skating on thin ice if you did, Totie. Fat is an absolutely essential part of a well-rounded diet and is found in foods such as milk, cheese, nuts and meat. Certain vitamins—A, D, E and K—cannot be absorbed by the intestines without fat in the diet.

High-fat foods also provide energy. Carbohydrates are the main energy source in your diet but fats also serve as fuel, particularly in long-distance and endurance sports. So while you shouldn't eat a lot of fat, don't cut it completely out of your diet.

If you want to see for yourself how fat provides energy, I'll send you an experiment you can do at home. Thanks for calling.

Well listeners, I'm afraid that's all the time I have for tonight. Please tune in next week when *The Sport of Munching* will ask, ''Does eating red vegetables help you to beet the odds?''

Totie's fat-finding experiment

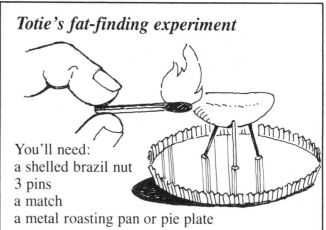

You'll need:
a shelled brazil nut
3 pins
a match
a metal roasting pan or pie plate

1. Ask permission to use the match.
2. Put the pan in the sink.
3. Stick the pins into the nut to make a tripod, as shown, and sit it in the pan.
4. Light the match and hold the flame to the nut until it catches fire. How long does the nut burn? Why does it keep burning so much longer than you think it would?

The fat in the nut provides the fuel for the fire, just as it would provide fuel for your muscles.

ANSWERS

That Sinking Feeling, page 44:

1. baked beans 11 g; 2. shredded wheat biscuits
6.1 g; 3. raw carrot 3.7 g; 4. apple 3.1 g; 5. whole
wheat bread 2.4 g; 6. white bread 0.8 g; 7. grapes
0.4 g; 8. egg 0 g.

Paper Puzzlers, pages 78-79:

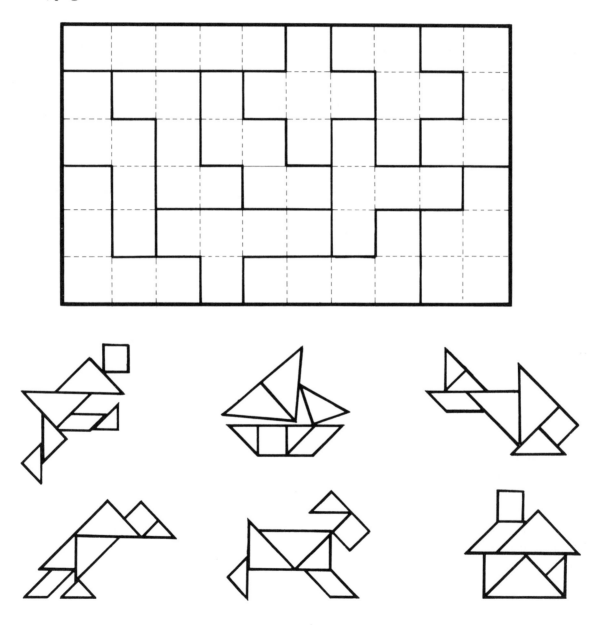

INDEX